THE
WHO DOES MORE
WAR

a guide to help couples
develop realistic expectations
and navigate inevitable
conflict after baby

JENNIFER GILL ROSIER, PH.D.
Associate Professor, James Madison University
Director, www.RelationshipsLoveHappiness.com

Front cover design by Jennifer Gill Rosier, Ph.D.
Interior book design by Jennifer Gill Rosier, Ph.D.
Edited by Martha Isom, M.A.

Like my book? Check out The RLH Project's website at www.RelationshipsLoveHappiness.com or Instagram page @RelationshipsLoveHappiness

The Relationships, Love, Happiness Project is a multi-faceted outreach project aimed at encouraging happy, healthy romantic and parent-child relationships.

Book printed in the United States of America
First printing: June 2020

For Wesley

I wouldn't want to do this completely
unpredictable parenthood thing with anyone else

Table of Contents

Introduction

Having a baby is supposed to be this wonderfully magical time in your life when the world stands still and you get to bask in the glory that is a precious, itty-bitty human being... right? Well, sorry to break it to you, but adding a new person to your life isn't always all it's cracked up to be. Don't get me wrong; there will be times where you'll be so filled with happiness that you won't want the moment to end. You won't be able to imagine loving another person as much as your tiny human and everything else in your life will begin to seem... well... insignificant at best. You'll have this overwhelming desire to spend every waking moment staring at, talking to, talking about, playing with, and caring for your new bundle of joy.

BUT (and that's a BIG but) while it can be filled with immense feelings of delight, it's also one of the most stress-inducing times in your life. In fact, studies have reliably documented a decline in marital satisfaction across the transition to parenthood[1], particularly for wives[2].

Whether it's your first child or your seventh, being a parent to a little person is stressful. I know- my husband and I have four kiddos: Gavin, Vivian, Paxton, and Rex. With all of the diaper changing, holding, feeding, rocking, shhh-ing, and worrying that takes place in those first few months (and years!), it's difficult to deal with all of the other stuff going on in your day-to-day. On top of the insanely different routine you're trying to adjust to, the hormones violently pumping through your body can make you feel like a complete crazy person. One minute, you're staring at your sleeping babe with feelings of pure happiness. And then the next minute, you're crying hysterically at the latest ASPCA commercial (Damn you, Sarah McLachlan!). Still only a minute later, you're viciously snapping at your mother-in-law for doing who the hell knows (more on this later). Oh yeah, and that new black hole in your wallet can most definitely cause you to wonder how you thought you could handle this new venture in the first place. And unfortunately, many women also experience post-partum depression on top of it all.

Researchers have identified a variety of factors contributing to this post-baby marital decline, including changing roles and responsibilities of spouses[3], increase in family stress[4], increase in marital conflict and decrease in positive spousal interactions[5], feelings of chaos[6], and violations of expectancies about parenthood[7] (all of which will be discussed at some point in this book).

The fact of the matter is that having a baby does a number on your capacity to feel normal. If you've already experienced the joy of becoming a new parent, you know exactly what I'm talking about. And if you're gearing up for this new journey, get ready for seemingly insignificant things to push your ass right off the deep end.

Furthermore, some people have this cockamamy idea that having a baby can save their failing relationship, increase feelings of intimacy in their distant relationship, or make them happier than they ever could imagine with their current unhappy relationship. And for some of you, having a baby *will* make you feel closer and happier with your spouse and relationship. But the key here is to *begin* this journey with a ridiculously strong bond. Those of you who are hoping to fix something, fill a void, or rekindle feelings in your relationship should probably steer away from baby-making as a solution to your problems. Having a child will not fix anything. In fact, it will likely create several new problems in your partnership.

The ugly truth is that having kids can end relationships and ruin marriages. The stress from all of the new responsibilities and the hours and hours taken away from the alone time you once had with your partner can put a serious strain on even the healthiest of relationships.

Having a baby is trying. You have to *really* love, and maybe more importantly *really* LIKE, the person who you have a baby with because even the most secure relationships are tested when a child is thrown into the picture.

The good news is that you can avoid some (but certainly not all) of these conflict-inducing problems simply by learning about the common arguments that new parents face, adjusting your expectations, and practicing some conflict deescalating techniques. Recognizing that these conflicts are completely normal can not only help you feel saner when they actually surface, but just by knowing what to expect, you can begin to create plans for dealing with these issues when the time to deal with them arises.

That's the plan for this book. I hope that you can learn about some of the things that couples with babies and young children typically argue about so that you can be prepared to combat these metaphorical "wars" when they happen. I'll also describe some research-based techniques and skills that you can implement into your daily interactions during this difficult life transition. And lastly, I'll embellish the advice with stories from my own life (Like I said, I'm married with four children) sprinkled throughout.

"I want to do life with you. I want to do the fun stuff, the adventurous stuff, and the shitty stuff. You're the only person I want to do the shitty stuff with."

Dr. Jennie Rosier

@RelationshipsLoveHappiness

Chapter One:
Here's the Thing About Expectations

It's 7 o'clock in the morning and I'm trying to get a few chores done before I leave thirty minutes later to take our four children to school and myself to work. I walk into our laundry room (as I typically do) and lift up our washer machine lid to see if the clothes need to be started or switched and … I'm HIT in the face with an awful smell. For some reason, I lean in to smell it again.

YUCK!

I know exactly what it is.

"Who peed in my washer machine?!" I yell.

But you see, this was really a rhetorical question- as I knew exactly who the culprit was. Some would call our oldest son, Gavin, "an experimenter" and others would call him a "person who doesn't give a shit about his mother's things." You know, to each their own. So, what was his reasoning for this atrocity?

"You never told me I couldn't."

And that sums up Gavin's reasoning for lots of the destructive things he does. Needless to say, we now have very specific rules in our house about where you're allowed to pee-

1. You cannot pee on each other.
2. If you're inside, you have to pee in the toilet.
3. If you're outside, you cannot pee where we walk or play.

I can honestly say that I *never* expected that my life with children was going to be filled with so many specific rules about pee.

But, here we are.

When people hear that I'm a relationship expert, they immediately start asking me for advice. Like right away. It's a bit odd.

I'm all, "I study the communication skills used to maintain romantic and parent-child relationships" and people are all, "How do I get my husband to do the dishes?" and "How do I get my baby to sleep through the night?"

Unfortunately, my answer to both of those questions is usually, "Ha! I'm not a magician!" Then the conversation typically turns to talking about why marriage and parenting are so {insert adjective here}.

One of my favorite things to then talk about is expectations—how we develop them, how they impact our communication in relationships, and how we can cope with them. You see, unrealistic expectations can cause serious issues in our lives. If we expect life to be one way and it's not, we might question if we're doing something wrong, argue with people in our lives about our mismatched expectations, or even quit something (school, a job, or a marriage) because it doesn't feel the way we expected it to feel.

As humans, we all want to know what's going to happen next. You want to know about little stuff like what you're going to eat for dinner or how your day is going to go tomorrow. And you want to know about big things like what it's going to be like when your next big life event happens- going to college, getting a new job, tying the knot, or having kids. Knowing what life is going to be like helps us reduce uncertainty, navigate our world with less stress, and feel a sense of calm. We are very motivated to reduce uncertainty.

We develop expectations throughout our lives to help us cope with this uncertainty. We base these expectations on lots of things. Three of them are below.

First, our relationships with other people shape our expectations. As we go through life and interact with lots of different people, we develop mental frameworks (or internal working models) in our brains that inform how we view ourselves (positively or negatively), how we view other people (positively or negatively), and how we view relationships with others (valuable and should be sought out or worthless and should be avoided). And these internal working models start to develop at birth.

Parents who quickly respond and consistently communicate with their children in a loving, sensitive, emotionally available manner create internal working models in their children's brains that tell them that they are loved and loveable, that other people are typically good-intentioned and capable of being trusted, and that they should create relationships with others because it is rewarding. Unfortunately, when parents do not communicate with their children this way—maybe they're completely unresponsive and even neglectful towards their children OR sometimes they're sensitive to their child's feelings and other times dismissive or aggressive towards their child's feelings, the internal working models created can potentially cause children to view themselves negatively and/or to either feel anxiety about or avoidance towards other people and the world.

This whole idea is at the foundation of attachment theory[8], which broadly explains how the bond between a child and their primary caregiver(s) impacts how that child's internal working models are developed.[9] Based on the sensitivity and consistency of caregiver responses, attachment foundations[a] are developed. Around 18 months of age (some researchers argue up to 3 years), the patterns of behavior that created attachment bonds with primary caregivers can help babies develop an attachment foundation. Children then tend to carry this attachment foundation with them throughout life; impacting how

> Attachment in early childhood with a primary caregiver has been shown to impact the way that you form, maintain, and even end friend, family, and romantic relationships later in life.
>
> (Bowlby, 1973; 1980)

---

[a] Most academic research would call this an "attachment style," but I like to call initial attachment an "attachment foundation" because I believe it better explains early attachment is an extremely important, yet completely malleable and ongoing, part of human development.

they start, maintain, and end friendships, family relationships, and romantic relationships with others.

All of those future relationship experiences also have the potential to impact our attachment. For example, if you have negative experiences with important people in your life betraying or abandoning you, you might begin to expect that people are not trustworthy or that relationships are not reliable. Conversely, if you have emotionally fulfilling relationships, your attachment security might be strengthened; causing you to expect people to get along with you, be good-intentioned, and relationships to be rewarding experiences that you want to participate in.

In sum, our early attachment foundation and later attachment style impacts how we view ourselves, choose to communicate with others, view the intentions of other people, and react to everyday stress or severe trauma. The internal working models developed cause us to expect certain things from ourselves, other people, and relationship experiences. This whole idea is summed up in the quote from Peggy O'Mara, "The way we talk to our children becomes their inner voice." Your inner voice guides your expectation development like a steering wheel.

> "The way we talk to our children becomes their inner voice."
>
> –Peggy O'Mara
> Parenting Expert & Editor of
> *Mothering Magazine*

Our third child, Paxton, is a "wanderer." For the longest time, when we would go to local events, Paxton would… wander. He'd be with us one minute and then he'd be gone. I know; it was super scary. But it also, in my opinion, said something about his internal working model about other people. We'd look around and find him with some new friends or even with another family doing a craft. I'd say, "Pax, we were looking for you. You can't go away from us like that." And he'd say, "Meet my new friends! This is Jake! Jake's mom is helping me pick paint for this rock I get to decorate!" See, in Paxton's eyes, people are good-intentioned. He honestly expects that he could be friends with anyone and that people aren't going to hurt him. We've since gotten him to stay closer when we're out in public, but he still generally looks at other people in the world through his precious little rose-colored glasses.

Our expectations are further informed when we watch people close to us interact with each other. Observing your parents, grandparents, aunts and uncles, or friends' parents communicate with one another fuels your expectations about how married people should (or maybe shouldn't) behave. Ideally, we all have excellent relationships to model, but unfortunately, this is not always the case. Imagine that you grew up in a house where you had a front row seat to two people who mocked one another incessantly or who yelled profanities at one another when they argued. You might grow up believing that this kind of conduct is a relationship expectation, which could either cause you to be pleasantly surprised when you have a partner who doesn't engage in that kind of destructive behavior or it could cause you to stay with a partner who does engage in destructive communication because "that's just the way it is."

Since we all have a distinctly unique life experience and perspective, we also all have diverse expectations about what life is supposed to be like. Clearly, this difference can cause serious problems and conflict when two individuals fall in love and decide to share a life together. You know, a life filled with stress.

A second, and sometimes extremely heavy, influencer on our expectations is the media. We watch television shows and movies, go on social media, and read books and articles written by opinion leaders and experts to find out what to expect. Hell, there's a whole multi-million dollar *What to Expect* empire selling millions of books to soon-to-be-parents around the world.

The media is everywhere.

Whether you like to want to believe it or not, famous television and movie couples have a significant impact on our expectations about how we should find a partner, communicate and interact with each other once we're connected to someone, and how we should feel in relationships[10].

We want to see if the connection that we have with our significant other measures up to our expectations. Maybe you watched a lot of *Roseanne*, *Everybody Loves Raymond*, or *Malcolm in the Middle* and you developed an expectation that a wife is destined to nag everyone in her family every single day of her life. Or maybe you watched a lot of *Married with Children* or *Sopranos* and you developed an expectation that men should not only not express their emotions, but also that they should degrade other people. Or worse, maybe you were obsessed with a few Disney princesses (#triggerwarning) and you developed an expectation that women can only truly be happy when a man saves her from her previous life (Think: Cinderella, Ariel, or Snow White). Even worse than that, maybe you began to expect that a woman can and should change a man; molding him into the man they want them to be even if the man is verbally or physically abusive (Think: Belle from *Beauty and the Beast*). Typical relationships found in the media create a skewed perception and then unrealistic expectations of what relationships in the real world should or should not be. Interestingly, the influence that the media has on the development of our expectations is exacerbated when what we see in the media is remotely similar to our actual life experiences.

> The media significantly impacts our expectations about how we should find a partner, communicate and interact with each other once we're connected to someone, and how we should feel in relationships.
>
> (Buckingham & Bragg, 2003; Chernin & Fishbein, 2007; Westman, Lynch, Lewandowski, & Hunt-Carter, 2003)

I remember growing up watching *Home Improvement* with Tim Allen. They had a busy house with three boys who would frequently get into trouble and a mom and dad who were navigating their lives raising these boys while simultaneously keeping their marriage together, maintaining adult friendships (especially their helpful, advice-giving neighbor), restoring various vehicles, and the dad starring in a low-key television program with his friend. I loved this show. My parents loved this show. So, it was definitely a show we watched a lot. And I always felt like I could relate to it. I didn't have any brothers (I had one sister), but my dad was a hilarious, fun-loving car guy (so was the dad, Tim) and my mom was definitely the house and kid manager (like the mom on the show, Jill). My parents were also really playful together; teasing each other a lot like Tim and Jill. And they were loving towards their kids; always supporting them and loving them unconditionally no matter what crazy shit the kids put them through. My parents worked really hard at making me feel special, loved, and lovable. I recognize and appreciate it. Probably the part that was the most relatable to me, though, was that Tim was such a fun dad. He joked around, he told stories, and he was just a great guy who made you want to be around him. Tim and my dad were quite similar in these ways. I subsequently developed an expectation that all dads are goof balls and that dads are really just an "extra kid" for the mom.

As you can probably guess, this expectation was a difficult one for me to overcome when my husband (who became a father to our children) was not exactly like this prototype that I developed in my head. Not in a bad way; just in a different way. A different way that I happen to love a whole lot.

The point is that if I wasn't able to let go of that expectation (whether it was good or bad; realistic or unrealistic), it could have caused miscommunication or conflict in my marriage. As mentioned previously, expectations help us lower our anxiety about the future and better navigate our lives, but they can also be restricting if we are not adaptable when things don't go as planned.

The media's influence doesn't stop with television and movies.

We also look at people on social media to compare our lives to theirs; developing even more expectations about our future. Search the hashtag #Parenting on Instagram and you'll find millions of images of some perfectly coordinated professional-grade family photos or some happily smiling children hugging one another with some stupid caption like, "If you think my hands are full, you should see my heart." Well, I call bullshit. What many of us forget is that Instagram and Facebook are filled with individuals who are posting their highest quality photos from mostly the best parts of their lives. The majority of posts are typically about love and togetherness and are rarely about any of the hard stuff. These images seep into our expectations about what relationships or parenthood is supposed to be like. And many times, this expectation is unrealistic at best.

My favorite (and by favorite, I clearly mean most hated) parenting posts are the photos of parents lovingly doing a craft project with their well-dressed, smiling children. They're carefully gluing their tiny pieces of paper together, painting without mixing any of the colors... and did I mention that they're all <u>smiling</u>? Seeing these images over and over could easily begin to cause onlookers to develop an expectation that this is normal. Well, it's not. Come to my house during craft time and it looks like a nuclear bomb went off where the warhead was filled with rainbow glitter and tiny shards of construction paper. And we're not smiling. Mostly because I'm yelling at one or all of our four beautiful children to stop throwing glue sticks at each other or drawing on the table or painting the dog's face or purposefully spilling the paint water so it ruins one of their sibling's artwork. It's stressful. And even though I am currently writing a chapter about expectations, how they become unrealistic, and how they can mess with your current life experience, in those moments, I **still** think to myself, "Why can't our craft time be like other people's craft time? Why can't we ENJOY EACH OTHER WHEN WE CRAFT LIKE ALL THOSE OTHER PEOPLE?!"

A third influencer on our expectation development is our culture. Culture tells us what is good and bad, right and wrong, worthless and valuable. Don't get me wrong, we're fully capable of making our own decisions. But what culture does is it tells you that in order for you to succeed and experience benefits in our culture, doing/believing in/agreeing with A, B, and C will help you.

For example, public speaking skills are highly valued in the U.S. This should be clear to you—we require most if not all college students in the US to take a public speaking course, we have thousands of books dedicated to the subject, and we have an entire field of study where thousands of researchers examine public speaking skills, strategies, and outcomes. The point is that we applaud people who can speak in front of an audience with polished conversational delivery, inspiring vocal variety, and clear organization and we make fun of people who… struggle (Think: Obama giving a speech vs. George W. Bush giving a speech). People who hone their skills are expected to achieve greatness; whatever that means. This doesn't mean that everyone in the U.S. culture is a good public speaker. Far from it. It just means that people who have polished this valuable skill tend to experience certain societal benefits and people who have a hard time speaking in front of an audience don't experience those benefits. This cultural value causes us to develop expectations about how people will treat effective public speakers and it encourages some of us to want to achieve that goal. Thus, we're inundated with messages from our culture throughout our lives that tell us what to expect.

Taken together, our relationship experiences, exposure to the media, and cultural values all combine to seriously impact what we expect out of life.

Sometimes these expectations help us. Let's say you have an expectation that people are generally good intentioned. This increases your likelihood to want to start and maintain relationships with other people. If you believe that people are good, you probably don't have many trust issues. You're also probably more willing to self-disclose, you're more interested in getting closer when you're in a relationship, and you probably don't think people are out to get you. Or let's say that you have an expectation about what a toxic relationship looks like. And then you're suddenly in one. You'll probably be more capable of realizing what's going on and get out. These expectations can improve your life experience.

But sometimes, our expectations can hurt us. Imagine you have really high expectations for a for potential romantic partner. I'm not talking high expectations like you're just not willing to settle. I'm talking about when your expectation list is so long or so specific that it causes you to not get involved with people because you never find anyone good enough or it causes you to end a relationship at the first sign of conflict because you don't think it should be that way. That's when expectations can mess with us a bit.

Expectations can also cause conflict when you're in a healthy relationship. It could be because you expect different things or because one of you copes better with the violation of your expectations or because you both didn't expect something to happen and neither of you know how to cope with the violation... separately or together.

I'm not talking about serious, dire life events that shock you to your core. Those things are important, but they don't happen on a daily basis. I'm talking about everyday bullshit. For instance, I didn't expect that I would have to wipe my kids' butts years after they were potty trained. Why doesn't anyone talk about that?! I think most people think: diapers for 2-3 years and then when they're potty trained, you're done. You're not. You still have to help wipe. For. Years. One of our kids went to kindergarten not knowing how to effectively wipe his own ass. So... he just didn't.

I can't tell you how many times my husband and I have looked at each other and said something like, "I definitely didn't think it would be like this."

Whether it's about marriage or parenthood, our expectations don't always match up with reality. And this can cause conflict, resentment, or even break-up or divorce. And let me tell you... kids seriously complicate things.

So what can you do?

The first thing you can do is get more realistic expectations. Talk to people who have experienced what you hope to and ask them what it's really like. Tell them to be real with you. You know, a lot of times, we think to ourselves, "I don't remember my parents having this hard of a time with us when we were kids." Well guess what—you didn't know your parents when they had small children. By the time you were actually noticing their parenting skills (or lack thereof), you were way past the newborn, toddler, or probably even elementary school age. Talking to people who are experiencing the life stage that you're going into, reading books like this one, or taking a parenting course can all help you develop more realistic expectations.

Second, avoid creating expectations based on the media. Disney hasn't taught us much about what real life is like. End of story.

Third, talk about what you expect with others and listen to what people who are involved in your life expect. Especially your partner. What do you both expect dating to be like? What do you expect marriage to be like? What do you expect parenthood to be like? And since we're on the subject, what's your plan for when baby arrives? How do you plan to deal with all of the new tasks you're acquiring? What kind of parents do you want to be? How can you both achieve that goal? Clearly, there is no way for you to fully prepare for parenthood, but having these conversations can be extremely helpful. To help you move this preparation process along, I have a long list of conversation starters in the back of this book. Pick a few questions over dinner each night and have fun!

Lastly, and this is probably the most important part, be flexible when things don't turn out the way you expected. Understand that everyone is different. Every relationship is different. And every kid is different. Many babies don't sleep through the night for months or even years, childhood tantrums can last well into their elementary school years, and early eaters love throwing food more than consuming food. Not being able to adapt to what parenthood throws at you can cause real problems in your relationship with the person you created this precious little hellion with.

I can honestly tell you that my husband and I thought we were ready. We read tons of books, talked to friends who were already parents, and took prenatal classes. We also had LOOOONG discussions throughout our nine-year pre-children life where we talked about how we wanted to raise our children. We would see other people with kids acting in ways that we didn't agree with and we would not only heavily judge those parents, but we would also swear that we would never let our kids do something like *that*.

We. Were. Ready.

And then, we got married, moved 13 hours away from all of our friends and family, and had boy/girl twins in 2009.

Holy. Hell. We were NOT ready.

We have since had two more children; totaling four. Four. And I can honestly tell you that we were not adequately prepared for large chunks of this whole "raising humans" thing.

> The overwhelming feelings individuals feel in parenthood often causes them to feel uncertain about their parenting abilities.
>
> (Belsky & Kelly, 1994; Cox et al., 1999; Weigel & Martin, 2004)

Well, the good news is that there is actually no way for **anyone** to fully prepare oneself for the inevitable trials and tribulations of parenting. If you feel like you don't know what the hell you're doing sometimes, YOU ARE NOT ALONE. In fact, one study asked participants to describe the first year of parenthood and the large majority of people called it *overwhelming*. This oftentimes causes parents to feel moderate to extreme uncertainty about their ability to cope with and even enjoy this new adventure[11].

Subsequently, uncertainty can lead new parents to seek out parenting advice[12] from friends and family, doctors, parenting books, or Facebook[13]. And even when new parents are not actively seeking out advice, they are still being inundated with, many times unsolicited, parenting advice[14].

Lucky for you, I'm not going to suffocate you with a bunch of parenting advice (there are dozens of other books that will do that). Instead, I'm going to focus on your relationship with your partner. I hope to help you prepare for all of the annoyance, frustration, and conflict you'll inevitably experience with your partner during this totally magical, yet extremely maddening, time of your life by describing some of the most common things that parents argue about. There's something about having a helpless little sack of sugar in your house that causes people to say things they wouldn't normally say to each other, fight about things they never fought about before, and get agitated over things they normally wouldn't care about. Learning about the kinds of things that couples typically argue over can help you create a plan for how you're going to deal with these issues when they arise.

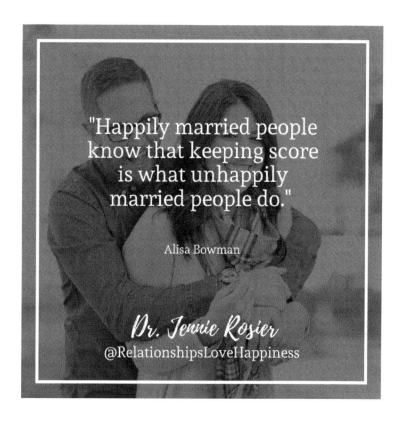

"Happily married people
know that keeping score
is what unhappily
married people do."

Alisa Bowman

Dr. Jennie Rosier
@RelationshipsLoveHappiness

Chapter Two:
The "Who Does More" War

If you live with your partner, you probably already feel like you've got this one in the bag. And you might. But having a baby significantly increases the number of chores you have to complete on a month-to-month, week-to-week, and day-to-day basis. So, you'll likely need to sort things out again. And if you're anything like the 10-years-ago version me, I would rather have just done it all than have an argument about how I felt like my husband wasn't doing his share. This caused me to feel overwhelmed and underappreciated at times; and that was BEFORE we had any children! We've since worked it out (for the most part), but I can't tell you how many little (and sometimes not-so-little) spats we've had about who is doing more when it comes to household chores and caring for our children.

> The division of household labor ranks third among topics most argued about in marital relationships.
>
> (Davidson & Moore, 1992)

When you have a baby, everything seems to triple. You have more laundry than you know what to do with, you're sweeping and vacuuming and mopping as much as possible to keep the floors clean for your itty-bitty (especially when they start crawling), and you're changing diapers around the clock. If you're nursing, well, it seems like all you do is have something (a baby or a pump) attached to your body and if you're formula-feeding, you're filling, mixing, heating, and washing bottles all freakin' day.

It's exhausting under normal circumstances, but did I mention that you're not doing *any* of this under normal circumstances? That's right—you're doing all of this extra work with very little SLEEP. You're drained, tired, and cranky. You're also trying to heal from the damage that pregnancy and delivery did to your body. To top it off, someone usually gets the short end of the stick in terms of the amount of work you take on. Oh, and that someone is stereotypically going to be you.

One of the most confusing, but consistent findings, in the division of labor literature is that although dual-earner wives (women who work outside of the house) tend to perform two to three times more household labor than their working husbands, less than one third of these women report the allocation of tasks to be unfair[15]. This is likely due to all of those culturally-informed, stereotypical gender role expectations we bring with us into our relationships. I would venture to say that most women tend to expect that they will do more of the household work, but only up to a certain amount. That amount is important. And, that amount differs from woman to woman. You and your partner need to agree on this amount. When you disagree and you start to feel like you're doing more than you bargained for, conflict ensues.

I remember when our twins were born. They were born six weeks early, stayed in the NICU for 12 days, and then we got to bring home these two 4.5lb humans. By ourselves.

All we really knew how to do was to hold them nonstop. That was our parenting style: hold and rock, hold and sway, hold and feed, hold and swaddle. And that worked for a while. But it didn't help our house stay clean or the dishes get done. We had a lot of discussions about who needed to do what. I needed my husband to pick up more of the chores during those first few months. And he did. When we had our third and fourth children, though, there was **so much more work**. And there were other children to care for this time around. It wasn't as easy for my husband to pick up the slack while I was healing and giving most of my attention to our new little bundle because he had older children that needed his attention. To cope, we divided up the kids a lot.

"You take the twins and I'll take the two little boys," I would say. Or he'd suggest, "I'll get the older kids in the shower while you get the baby to sleep." There was a lot of juggling. A lot of bartering. A lot of compromise. But there was also a lot of both of us feeling like we were doing way more work than the other person. And a lot of ignoring the underlying issue that was pushing us apart. I remember my husband saying to me once, "I feel like I'm a single dad to three young kids who lives with this woman who has a baby. I get to hang out with her sometimes, but she's really busy. And because she's always tired and I like her, I end up doing most of the cooking and cleaning." It was a request for more equality *and* a bid for connection. A plea for connection. We had to do something to change the way we were divvying up the never-ending to-do list. We had conversations about how to fix this feeling we were both having that we were just a couple of roommates raising kids side-by-side. We decided that in order for us to feel more connected, we needed to (1) not split up the kids as consistently as we were splitting them up (I needed to be "in charge" of caring for the three older kids more and he needed to care for the baby more), (2) try to do some of the chores together instead of individually, and (3) spend more one-on-one time together. We also decided that the kids were old enough to take over a few of the chores—which actually helped more than we thought it would.

The point is that one of the more difficult adjustments during this life stage, in my opinion, is the massive extending of your to-do list.

When you bring a newborn home (whether it's your first or your sixth), there's an immediate influx of chores that have to be done to keep you and your baby happy and healthy. You

> Couples who share tasks exhibit more mutual control, like each other more, and are more committed to and satisfied with their relationship.
>
> (Stafford & Canary, 1991)

have to diaper, feed, soothe, carry, clean, rock, and shush your baby for hours on end most days. You also have a few vital doctor's appointments in those first few months that both your baby and you have to attend. And did I mention that your body is healing? Regardless of how you deliver, each method comes with its own set of recovery issues. Your body is in pain. And that's if everything goes as planned. Delivery complications can lead to even more pain, more doctor's appointments, and/or more time recovering than the average person. Those first 6 months after having a baby are hard.

Many of you will also have to deal with going back to work during this time. I'm always amazed, and deeply saddened, when I hear that women are going back to work as early as 6 weeks. It pains me to even think about it. Six weeks is not enough time for your body to heal. And it's definitely not enough time for you to have with your baby. While talking about the state of our failing U.S. maternity leave policies is not the purpose of this book, it's an issue of which we all should be concerned. Six weeks is not enough time. Hell, 12 weeks is not enough time. I was unbelievably fortunate to have 16 weeks off work with our twins, 10 weeks of pregnancy-induced bedrest plus 16 weeks off work for our third child, and six months off work for our fourth child. All paid with really great health insurance. Unfortunately, I am not anywhere near the norm. And many other countries have even better maternity (and paternity!) leave benefits than what I was able to experience. The system is broken. Do what you can to prepare. Figure out how you and your partner could shift your schedules or if you can save up extra time off (to add to your maternity leave if you have any). You might not believe it now, but for many women (clearly, not everyone), going back to work is devastating. Take as much time as you are able. You won't regret it. I digress, back to the *Who Does More War*.

The work doesn't just stop after the first few months. It changes. In some ways, the work gets easier and in other ways, the work gets a lot harder. Toddlers need to be followed or contained (for their safety once they become mobile), entertained and actually played with (ha!), fed multiple times a day, and repeatedly cleaned because they're super messy little people. And the crying. Oh, the crying. Dealing with the emotional breakdowns of little people can be one of the hardest "jobs" that many couples argue about.

Little kids (and many big kids!) cry multiple times a day. About anything and everything. Our third child, Paxton, use to cry incessantly most mornings because his shoes were not tied. But if you tried to help him, he would cry about you helping. So, he wanted his shoes tied, but you couldn't help, but he didn't know how to tie them, but you couldn't tie them for him, but they needed to be tied, but no one could do it. This lasted for a whole week before his tie shoes suddenly disappeared and he had Velcro shoes. The point is that toddlers and older kids cry about some of the most unreasonable things. Put that in your expectations. And dealing with this insanity is a major chore for parents that takes lots of patience and understanding and patience and then more patience.

Don't get me wrong, babies cry, too. But, at least for me (I understand that I'm abnormal), I don't get upset when babies cry. It's how they communicate. I see it differently. I'm not sure how, but I have a significant amount of patience with infants.

> Whines enter into a child's vocal repertoire with the onset of language, typically peaking between 2.5 and 4 years of age.
>
> (Borba, 2003; Sears & Sears, 1995)

Let me hear a four-year-old whine/cry uncontrollably about something that I view as insignificant or trivial and I'm triggered. I try really hard to maintain my calm, but after several minutes, my patience typically leaves my body and I become incapable of effectively supporting my child. Many times, I even lose my cool and verbally overreact. Interestingly, research has shown that lots of people have a similar outlook on infant crying and toddler whining as myself; with the majority of people perceiving toddler whining as significantly more annoying than infant crying[16]. This doesn't mean, however, that most people have a ton of patience with infant crying. Instead, it means that toddler whining is simply considered *more* annoying.

My husband has less patience based on what caused the whining and crying in the first place. He also has less patience than me with infant crying. He almost always starts off calm, but it doesn't last very long depending on the reasoning behind the upset. The point is that everyone has their own set of triggers and their own stress threshold that they bring to parenthood. Figuring out what your own are and what your partner's are can help you both work through this never ending job of calming down small people.

There's actually been some interesting research on this. One study, published in the *Journal of Social, Evolutionary, and Cultural Psychology*, revealed that toddler whining and infant crying are two of the most effective ways to distract adults when they are trying to perform an elementary task[17]. In this study, adults were less able to concentrate when listening to these two sounds than when listening to other seemingly annoying sounds such as the screeching sound of sawing wood, fingernails on a chalkboard, and loud machine noise. So, you're taking on all of these new tasks, not experiencing much quality sleep, and the crying and whining being produced by this precious little person you willingly created is making it extremely difficult for you to focus on anything; even stuff you used to consider easy.

The often relentless crying in the beginning of parenthood can make even the most calm and patient individuals feel as though they're losing their minds. And then as the weeks turn into months and the months turn into years, the incessant whining kicks into high gear. And *all* kids whine. There is no avoiding this phase of childhood. Anything that annoys, upsets, saddens, frustrates, or angers a child can cause them to whine about it. For example, lots of our child-related whining centers around food. They whine about what they want to eat, what we're giving them to eat, what they don't want to eat, the amount of time it takes for me to make the food that they want to eat, the amount of time it takes them to actually eat, and the texture of the food they have agreed to eat. And that could all be whined about during one meal. And it could all come from one child. It can be an extremely frustrating chore that parents have to deal with (or at least endure).

You and your partner are going to need to learn how to cope with two of the most annoying sounds on this planet living in your house. Helping your child get through all of their big, and small, emotions and figuring out which one of you is going to do the calming plays a huge role in the *Who Does More War*.

Once pre-K or elementary school begins, you start to breathe a bit because they're doing a lot of things on their own and they've hopefully gotten control over *some* of their meltdowns (but not always- our third child had complete mental breakdowns for YEARS). But then you're thrown into the world of school closings, early releases, and two-hour delays. How are you going to deal with these childcare dilemmas; especially the unpredictable ones (you know, the ones that you get a text about at 5am)? If you both are employed outside of the home, deciding whose job is more flexible can be tricky. Are you going to switch back and forth between the two of you taking off work when delays and school closings require your kids to stay home? Is one of you going to take control of this domain because you have a flexible job? Do you have childcare alternatives (like going to Grandma's house or to a childcare gym/center/etc.) available to you when kids are off school? What are your plans for the summer?

And don't get me started on extra-curricular activities. Most sports teams meet two or three times a week for practices and games and most other activities meet once a week. This isn't such a huge deal when you have one child in one weekly activity, but additional children in this stage can complicate your after-school and after-work plans (when you're already exhausted from the day of activities).

We had this stint for a few years that we affectionately called "the busy winter season." And it looked a little bit like this:

Mondays: Paxton and Rex went to Cub Scouts & Gavin went to Boy Scouts (in two different locations, at the same time of day)
Tuesdays: Paxton went to wrestling practice
Wednesdays: Vivian went to art club right after school
Thursdays: Vivian went to jump rope team practice right after school and then Gavin went to wrestling that evening
Fridays: NOTHING
Saturdays: Paxton went to wrestling practice– two of these Saturdays were entire-day wrestling tournaments for all three boys
Sundays: Gavin went to wrestling practice

This doesn't even include all of the random doctor and dentist appointments, performances, parties, or family gatherings we somehow squeezed into our already hectic calendar. It was a tough few winters. Managing who would drive and who would pick up each child at each time was a juggling act that I don't wish on anyone. We were extremely blessed to have my mom living nearby and being willing to pick up some of the driving. But even with the help, it caused conflict in our marriage if one of us thought we were doing more or if one of us didn't get their job done or if one of us complained while doing these tasks. It's easy to fall into this cycle of bitching and moaning when you're adding all of this new stuff to your schedule. But don't forget, you're willingly increasing the stress in your life; you aren't required to do any of this extra stuff as a parent. If your marriage or family are suffering because of your chaotic schedule, you have some control here. Even though your kids might be upset about taking a break from their sports team, keeping your family happy and healthy is much more important than little Jimmy playing basketball for three months.

> During the transition to parenthood, perceived unfairness of the division of labor predicts later marital conflict and marital dissatisfaction; especially for wives.
>
> (Grote & Clark, 2001)

Talk with your partner about how you plan to address this problem if and when it becomes an issue. Are you going to limit the number of activities your children can participate in? For instance, you might decide that each child can only participate in one activity at any given time. Are you going to place contingencies on extracurricular involvement? For example, maybe you decide that your child can only be involved in activities where they can carpool with another family in at least one direction. Are you going to be willing to stop an activity if it becomes too much for your family? These are important things to consider that go past the normal considerations about who is going to physically take your kids to all of their activities—you have to figure that out, too, by the way.

The fact of the matter is that having kids adds a ton of work to your already busy life—well, the life that you *thought* was busy. And, you have to figure out that new, ridiculously busy life with another person. A person who you're hopefully committed to and love a whole lot, but also a person who brings a completely different set of expectations, childhood baggage of their own, and perceptions about life experiences to the relationship.

Let's just talk about different expectations for a bit. The main set of expectations that mess with this war involves gender roles. If you and your partner have different gender role expectations (beliefs about what sorts of things men and women should and shouldn't do), the *Who Does More War* that happens in your house could be significantly intensified. I'm talking thermal nuclear level.

Some couples are perfectly fine with one person doing a lot more of the child-raising and household chores than the other partner, while other couples want everything to be equal; down to the smallest of tasks. The key is to hash these ideas out so that you're both on the same page. There's no right way divide work in a relationship. Instead, you need to recognize how important it is that as a couple, you come to a certain level of agreement on this issue. If you and your mate disagree about who should fill each role in your life together, you will likely experience a significant amount of conflict down the road.

We all come into relationships with ideas about how men and women should and should not behave and communicate. For instance, in some circles, people believe that women should stay at home and be primary caregivers for their children, while men should go to work and provide for their families. Other people expect that men should do certain "manly" chores like cutting grass, fixing things, and plunging toilets, while women should do more "feminine" chores like cooking meals, changing diapers, and cleaning the house. Still, other people have more fluid gender role expectations, with men and women doing chores they like or are good at more than what society has assigned then to do based on their sex. Again, there's no right or wrong way to divide up chores, but talking about what you expect is really important to maintaining the peace.

If you fundamentally want your life after kids to be one way and your mate expects your life to be another way, someone is going to not get what they want and resentment can eventually build up.

Further complicating the *Who Does More War* is that no matter what (no matter who is actually doing more), no one ever wins this war. It's very difficult to listen to the other person's perspective when you feel like your effort is being attacked. And based on each person's individual set of expectations, both of you will always feel like you're doing a lot. One of you could say that you're doing A, B, and C (implying that the other is not) and then the other person could easily respond with the fact that they do D, E, and F. Defensiveness becomes rampant during the discussion of this war. The deliberation stops being about who does more and what needs to change for the complainer to be happy and it becomes a petty tit-for-tat argument. At this point, there usually isn't anything that either of you can say to convince the other person that they are not pulling their weight.

"No one likes doing chores. In happiness surveys, housework is ranked down there with commuting as activities that people enjoy the least. Maybe that's why figuring out who does which chores usually prompts, at best, tense discussion in a household and, at worst, outright fighting."

–Emily Oster, Ph.D.
Professor of Economics,
Brown University

"I feed the baby 8-12 times a freaking day! For 10 to 40 minutes each time! The least you can do is change her diaper!" A typical response to this attack could be, "Are you kidding me?! I work for 10 hours every day to put food on our table and you get to hang out at home all day!" Well, shit. Let the tit-for-tat battle begin!

It's hard to come out of that altercation feeling good about your partner or yourself. This is why recognizing that this war is inevitable, adding it to your set of parenthood expectations, having a super clear discussion about it before baby arrives, and promising to check in with each other after baby is born is vital to creating a plan for the future. Expect to not be happy about the amount of work you feel like you're putting into your life as parents. Expect that your partner will feel like they're doing enough. Expect to feel like getting defensive is the only way out. Expect the *Who Does More War* to wreak havoc on your new life as parents.

Then, make a plan together for coping with it all. How do you want to bring up your concerns about feeling overworked or even taken advantage of? Should you bring up concerns as they're happening or do you want to try to wait until you've had some time to breathe? Do you want to create a code word or phrase that can make the starting of this discussion more light-hearted?

Researchers have examined the communication strategies that couples use when bringing up household work issues[18]. Some couples use more direct strategies (ex: clearly stating that you're not happy with the status quo) while others use more passive, indirect strategies (ex: leaving out the dirty dishes until it is clear that you're not going to clean them) to bring up feelings of unfairness regarding the division of duties. Unfortunately, research has also shown that women are much more likely to bring up the discussion; which indicates that the *Who Does More War* is also likely started by women. Clear, supportive, calm communication is critical for couples attempting to negotiate the divisions of household and childcare tasks. And talking about it before the diapers hit the fan is beneficial.

Whatever you do, try to avoid keeping score about who does more, because trust me, no one wins and it will just piss you off.

"You can't wait until you both have more time for sex because that day may never happen. Instead, you have to consciously set time aside for sex."

Dr. Jennie Rosier
@RelationshipsLoveHappiness

Chapter Three:
The "Why Don't You Want to BLEEP Me Anymore" War

Pregnancy does some pretty messed up (yet totally normal) things to a woman's body; most of which are TMI to discuss at length here (another topic for another book). One of the more prominent side effects of pregnancy (sometimes during, but mostly afterwards) is a woman's total lack of a sex drive. While it's not always this extreme (some women actually experience an increase in their sex drive!), most women experience some kind of lowered libido after having a child. And with many women, engaging in sexual activities with their partners is the absolute last thing on their mind.

This is largely due to the significant drop in estrogen and rise in prolactin and oxytocin that occurs after delivery. These hormones combine in interesting ways to impact the way you feel. The science here is fascinating. We know that hormonal changes occur during the postpartum period can contribute to decreased sexual desire and arousal[19]. Some of these changes take place within the amygdala, a structure in our brains that is related to both sex drive, emotion, and reward processing. Postpartum women have been shown to have decreased amygdala responsiveness[20]. So, we experience sexual desire and arousal when our amygdala is activated, but the hormones that rush through our bodies after delivery can make it difficult for this activation to occur. Thus, a good amount of your sexual desire and arousal depletion is completely out of your control.

> The hormones that rush through your body after delivery can make it extremely difficult for the part of your brain responsible for sexual desire to be activated.
>
> (Rupp, James, Ketterson, Senegelaub, Ditzen, & Heiman, 2013)

For many women, including myself, having a baby gives you a rush of happiness and feelings of elation while simultaneously causing you to completely lose it (either via sadness or anger) at the drop of a hat. You're so incredibly happy to finally have this new bundle in your arms, but you're also worried and stressed and overwhelmed. If you thought pregnancy did a number on your emotional state, just wait until those days and weeks after baby arrives. I clearly remember feeling bat-shit crazy. One minute, I would be over-the-moon happy and absolutely nothing could upset me and then the very next minute my ass would fall right off the deep end and I was screaming at my poor husband about who the hell knows what and nothing could calm me down. Except maybe a good cry. It's a roller coaster, really. A fun-filled, kind of scary, totally unpredictable roller coaster.

> Approximately 41% to 86% of women at the 3-month postpartum mark report at least one sexual dysfunction problem.
>
> (Barrett, Pendry, Peacock, Victor, Thakar, & Manyonda, 2000; Glazener, 1997; Hicks, Goodall, Quattrone, & Lydon-Rochelle, 2004; Leeman & Rogers, 2012)

These hormonal changes coupled with the constant contact with your baby can fill you up emotionally and physically; which could then cause you to not only forget about connecting with your partner, but it could actually make you not want to seek affection from your partner at all. This sensation has been referred to as feeling "touched out." You're holding, nursing, rocking, and hugging your baby sometimes all day long and just the thought of touching another human could feel excessive and undesirable. If this feeling persists, you could unconsciously (or consciously) be ignoring your partner for weeks or months and this disconnection could easily cause serious problems in your relationship.

Interestingly though, there are some women who experience an *increase* in sexual desire after baby arrives. Your new hormone cocktail could actually make you feel *more* aroused. I don't personally know any of these women, but apparently, they exist.

If you feel like your sex life is suffering after baby, you're not alone. Several research studies have shown that approximately 41% to 86% of women at 3 months postpartum report at least one indicator of sexual dysfunction[21]; which include problems with desire, arousal, orgasm, and pain. And at 6 months postpartum, these rates are still as high as 64%[22]. Not only do postpartum mothers often cite problems with vaginal pain[23], dryness[24], and a decrease in sexual arousal[25], but women also tend to complain about a decrease in feelings of relational closeness with their partner[26].

Clearly, there are many reasons for this decrease in sexual activity. After the six-week mark (when most women are cleared to start having sex again), sexual pain is a frequently named cause[27]. Whether you have a vaginal or cesarean delivery, sexual pain is extremely common. (Put this in your set of expectations!) Some women experience moderate to high pain the first few times they engage in intercourse and others experience pain for the duration that they decide to breastfeed. In fact, breastfeeding can negatively impact vaginal dryness[28], fatigue[29], and hormonal changes (elevated prolactin and lower androgens)[30], which can lower one's desire to want to engage in anything related sex. If you breastfeed for a year (or more), this could be an issue for a while.

There's also this pesky tunnel vision thing many women experience after having a baby. You're probably going to be thinking about, looking at, and talking about your baby most of the day. And, this is normal. Many, but certainly not all, women can become consumed with their new little cherub. This can make it difficult to think about, and especially do, anything else. Hopefully, you're consumed with happy thoughts, but you could also become consumed with worry. Either way, it can be difficult to plan for and engage in sexual activities with your partner. Even if you get started, many women have a difficult time shutting off their new mommy brain while they're having sex.

The worst side effect that some women unfortunately experience after having a baby is postpartum depression. In the year following the birth of a child, women can experience psychological well-being and a deep sense of meaning and joy while getting to know and care for their new baby. However, this is also a period of increased psychological vulnerability, where women can experience a range of mental health issues as well[31]. These feelings can range from normal mood changes all the way to serious symptoms that require hospitalization. Research has shown that while approximately 80% of women experience mild to moderate psychological distress, 15–30% of women will have symptoms which meet diagnostic criteria, with the most frequent mental health issues being depression, anxiety, posttraumatic stress disorder, and eating disorders, as well as the possibility of psychosis[32].

> 15%-30% of women will experience more severe mental health issues including, depression, anxiety, PTSD, eating disorders, and/or psychosis.
>
> (Gawley, Einarson, & Bowen, 2011; Goodman & Santangelo, 2011; McBride & Kwee, 2016; Zaers, Waschke, & Ehlert, 2008)

Then there's the body image issue. It's no secret that having a baby changes the way your body looks and feels. There's weight gain and loss, vaginal changes, hair loss, stretch marks, changes in breast shape and size, abdominal muscle separation, varicose veins, wider hips, hemorrhoids... the list can go on and on. And for many women, these changes can impede on their sex life. Research has found that women tend to have serious concerns about their body image especially in the 12 months following the birth of a child and that these concerns can often cause women to refrain from engaging in sexual activity[33].

If the part of your brain responsible for your sex drive isn't being activated, you're more exhausted than you ever thought was possible, you feel "touched out," you're constantly thinking about your baby, you feel physical pain during sex, and you don't feel too great about the way you look... well, it's going to be extremely difficult for you to get in the mood and stay in the mood for any amount of time. The cards are stacked against you.

The general consensus here is that after a couple has a baby, they typically have less sex and the sex that they are having is less satisfying. This negatively impacts their romantic relationship. Remember- this is happening on top of all the other shit that's happening. Your sex life is suffering on top of all of the extra tasks on your to-do list, on top of all of the worrying you're doing for that new little person you created, and on top of all of the hormones that are surging through your body making you moody, sad, and aggressive all at the same exact time. It's a lot.

> First-time fathers report a significant decrease in relationship satisfaction during the first year of their new baby's life.
>
> (Condon, Boyce, & Corkindale, 2004)

This problem, unfortunately, can continue (sometimes getting worse) for several months or years after your baby is born. A change in your sex life can cause a lot of conflict in your relationship; especially if your pre-pregnancy relationship was filled with frequent and satisfying sex. For many men (clearly, not all men), sex is an extremely important component of their feelings of relationship security and self-worth. A sudden lack of sex can cause even the most secure men to feel anxious or even fearful about their relationship.

Studies have shown that first-time fathers typically report a significant increase in dissatisfaction with their romantic relationships during the first year after baby[34]. And, the main cause of this dissatisfaction is a lack of physical and emotional intimacy within the relationship. New fathers tend to cite their partner's loss of sex drive as one of the main contributors here. One study[35] conducted in-depth interviews with 6-month postpartum fathers and found that, in general, fathers were prepared for sexual intercourse to stop for several weeks immediately following the birth of their babies. But, this study also showed that fathers did not expect their sex lives to suffer as much as they were suffering after that period of time. Interestingly, fathers consistently claimed that they wanted to communicate more frequently about the intimacy issues they were experiencing with their partners. In fact, the study described it as a "huge need." Fathers also reported wishing they could get more physical touch, like hugging and snuggling, from their partners during these "dry spells."

Acknowledging your partner's feelings and explaining that it's not him (it's your hormones/tiredness/depression/physical pain) that's causing you to not be in the mood can help.

I think one of the most important discussions my husband and I had about this subject happened when I was pregnant with our third child, Paxton (second pregnancy because we had twins first). I remember feeling like we just brushed all of the frustration and conflict about sex under the rug when our twins, Gavin and Vivian, were born and we never really discussed anything. I wanted to have a clear discussion before our lives were complicated again with another baby. Something that has always stuck out in my husband's mind about that discussion was when I said to him, "I just need you to realize that my lack of affection or refusal of your sexual advances have nothing to do with you or how I feel about you and our marriage. Instead, it has everything to do with me, my hormones, my confidence, and my exhaustion. Try not to take it personally." This was a turning point for us. Then Paxton was born. I worked really hard at increasing physical touch with him, he worked really hard at understanding my emotional and physical state, and we both worked really hard at talking about our feelings as we were having them. It wasn't easy, but it was way better than the first pregnancy where we just ignored it all.

Be aware of your partner's point of view, validate his feelings, and try to increase your physical touch with him as much as you feel comfortable doing. And sometimes, a good old-fashioned make-out session is the only cure. Expressing your attraction to him is also something you're going to want to implement into your daily routine. And whatever you do, DO NOT act as if engaging in intimate activities with him is a chore. This can completely damage his confidence and can easily cause the two of you to drift apart. Trust me when I say that you do not want that to happen. Just keep reminding yourself that this phase of parenthood will pass.

Here's the kicker- yes, this phase of parenthood will pass. Your sex drive will return (maybe not all the way, but it will get better). Your ability to be sexually aroused will return. And you will have satisfying sex again. But, if you create patterns of disconnection, detachment, and distance in your relationship during this early phase that you both are not committed to breaking free from later, your sex life could continue to suffer. For years. You could easily drive a wedge between you and your partner. Getting stuck in a repetitive series of interactions with your mate where you don't connect with one another can be difficult to turn around.

> "Real life romance is fueled by a far more humdrum approach to staying connected. It is kept alive each time you let your spouse know he or she is valued during the grind of everyday life."
>
> –John Gottman, Ph.D.

You both have to be dedicated to reconnecting. You might have to force yourself a bit. That feeling is normal. If you want to keep your relationship going strong for years to come, working on your sex life is vital to attaining that goal.

Fortunately, one of the things that my husband and I have learned over the last decade or so is that there is absolutely NO SHAME in scheduling sex with one another. I'm serious. And here are three reasons why I believe that you and your partner should consider following suite.

Reason #1: You will always be busy.

Many times, couples will try and justify the fact that they're not having enough sex. And, one of the most common reasons is that one or both partners don't have enough time for sex. Life is hectic. Believe me, I get it. But I think it's important to realize that you will *always* be busy. Life is not going to magically slow down for you to have sex with your partner. And it sure as hell isn't going to slow down a few times a week. The take-home message: you can't wait until you have more time because that day may never happen. You have to consciously set time aside for sex.

Reason #2: Sex drives are not always in sync.

It is believed by many that both partners have to be completely "in the mood" to have sex, and especially to have *good* sex. Unfortunately, if you decide to wait until both you and your partner are sexually aroused and ready to get it on, you might just have to wait forever. People are different. You and your partner may not be on the same sexual clock as one another. I know, you probably feel like you *used* to share the same sexual wavelength, but another interesting thing about people is that they change. In particular, you and your partner's sex drives may change over time, which could allow you to get out of sync more often than you're used to. It's important to note that this discrepancy is *not* a sign of your relationship's imminent demise. Quite the contrary. It's actually your *response* to these changes that can help predict your future together. Having sex on a regular basis, regardless of how hot-and-heavy you're feeling at a particular moment, is a great response to this potential problem in the bedroom.

Reason #3: Sex is important!

I've written about this extensively in my other book (*Finding the Love Guru in You*) and I'll summarize it here: having sex, actually enjoying it, and especially orgasming multiple times a week is related to numerous physical, mental, and relationship benefits[36]. Specifically, researchers have discovered that engaging in these activities is associated with a longer lifespan[37], lower level of depression[38], increased self-esteem[39], and enhanced feelings of affection and closeness with a sexual partner[40] to name a few. Sex is important. Do whatever you can to make it happen in your relationship.

BENEFITS OF HAVING SEX, ENJOYING IT, & ORGASMING

PHYSICAL BENEFITS

-Reduction in the risk for and incidence of heart disease
-Decreased risk of prostate cancer
-Lower risk for and incidence of breast cancer
-Lower incidence of endometriosis
-Heightened ability to sleep
-Longer life

PSYCHOLOGICAL BENEFITS

-Decreased need for psychiatric medications
-Lower levels of depression
-Reduced feelings of stress
-Increased self-esteem
-Better quality of life

RELATIONSHIP BENEFITS

-Increased feelings of intimacy and closeness
-Higher levels of relationship satisfaction
-Longer relationships

This list was created from an article by Whipple, Knowles, & Davis (2007)

Creating a Schedule

Scheduling sex *around* your busy schedule probably won't work. If you already feel like you're too busy, then you will likely also feel like you're unable to find the time and you just won't schedule it. Similarly, trying to schedule based on the days when you think you might be turned on probably won't work either. If you haven't been able to sync up your sex drives yet, it will likely be very difficult to find an agreement for the future. Instead, begin by choosing a general time of day (i.e. morning before work, on your lunch break, before dinner, right after your kids go to sleep, or right before you and your partner go to sleep) that you both can agree on. Then, you can start choosing the days. Some couples like to pick specific days of the week, like Mondays, Thursdays, and Saturdays. While other couples may feel more comfortable picking a pattern of "sex days." For example, I know a couple who has sex every other day and then another couple who has sex every three days.

> Unfortunately, many couples are plagued with dissatisfying sex lives, with some marriages even becoming sexless (i.e. couples who engage in sex less than 10 times per year) overtime.
>
> (Dunn, Jordan, Croft, & Assendelft, 2002)

However you decide to work it out is up to you and your mate. Just be sure to work hard at sticking to it! Once you've chosen your days, plan to definitely have sex with your partner- almost no matter what. I know what you're thinking: what if you're sick on your sex day or what if something terrible happens on that day and you just can't concentrate? It's completely fine to skip a day here and there. Or factor in a few rejection cards for each of you to use as you please. It only becomes a problem when you and/or your partner begin to habitually skip days that you've set aside for sexual intimacy.

Interestingly, scheduling sex has helped a lot of couples light a spark in their relationships. Although it doesn't sound logical, there's something to say about knowing when it's going to happen.

The pressure of figuring out who is going to initiate and whether the initiator is going to be rejected become things of the past.

For many people, getting started is the hardest part. And, thinking about it all day could be a good thing! Fantasizing about what will happen before it happens could enhance the experience for both people.

Okay, let's say you get it—you believe that sex is important, you're comfortable talking about it with your partner, you want to do it, and you're even willing to create a schedule with your partner. But for whatever reason, you're still having a significant amount of trouble.

Next are eleven ways to boost your sexual desire (and yes, I'm fully aware that many of these things are near impossible to get done with a brand-new baby around, but when you're ready and more able, something on this list might help you want to get back in the bedroom more often).

11 WAYS TO BOOST YOUR SEXUAL DESIRE

GET ENOUGH SLEEP

Lacking the proper amount of sleep can negatively impact many parts of your life, including your libido. In addition, it's really hard to get excited about sex when you're exhausted. Try getting more sleep every night and see if you're more interested in getting it on. (I know this is difficult to do with a new baby, but maybe a nap during the day could help.)

EXERCISE

I know it's hard to believe, but exercising can actually give you more energy. And, if you exercise regularly, you'll begin to feel more confident with your body and you'll likely become more willing to show it off in between the sheets.

EAT HEALTHIER

Eating three balanced meals a day will make you look and feel great. And when you feel good, you'll have more energy and more confidence, which can help you get in the mood.

MASSAGE

Not only does massage have the ability to lower anxiety, alleviate pain, relax muscles, and increase joint mobility, but romantic, sensual massage can also increase intimacy and feelings of love between two lovers. So, make a sexy play list on your iPod and get ready rub hot oils all over your lover.

BE DANGEROUS

Sometimes a little danger can spark something in your relationship. Going skydiving, rock climbing, or ride some roller coasters and use the feelings of euphoria created by dopamine and adrenaline flowing through your body to create some excitement in the bedroom.

ROLE-PLAY

Role-playing is a great way to keep things interesting in your relationship, which is sometimes a cause of low sex drive. You could role-play at home or role-play out on a date. Role-playing is adventurous and a lot of fun. And, it could easily light a flame in your relationship.

TALK DIRTY

Men and women can both benefit from a little risqué conversation. Many times, dirty talk can make your mate feel desired, sexy, and naughty. All of which are great sensations to experience when you're getting ready to do the nasty.

USE SEX TOYS

Many times, sex toys are able to do things that humans are just incapable of doing. This is nothing to be ashamed of. If you or your partner has trouble orgasming or if you would like your orgasms to be even more intense than they already are, sex toys are a great way to achieve your goals. And, they're not just for women anymore. There are plenty of sex toys that help men achieve more pleasure, you just need to choose the one that's best for you.

SET THE MOOD

Getting out the candles, turning down the lights, and playing some soft music can all set the mood for love in your house. Doing these romantic things for your partner doesn't only have the ability to intensify sexual feelings, but they can also bring you closer as a couple.

ASK YOUR DOCTOR

If you feel like you have a physical problem that is causing you to have a low sexual desire, talk to your doctor. Sometimes, hormone imbalances, certain prescription drugs, anemia, diabetes, an actual sexual dysfunction, your blood pressure, specific types of cancer, particular STDs, or other physical ailments are the cause of a low libido. Get your annual physical and ask your doctor about whether some of these things could be causing your sexual desire problems.

CONSULT A THERAPIST

You and/or your partner may also want to talk to a therapist, psychiatrist, or counselor about your issues with sexual desire. Find a local practitioner, schedule an appointment, and work out your sexual desire difficulties with a professional.

Having some empathy with your partner is so important when dealing with the *Why Don't You Want to Bleep Me Anymore War*. Put yourself in your partner's shoes. How would you feel if your mate all of the sudden didn't want to have sex with you anymore? How would you feel you felt like your partner was annoyed (or disgusted) by you wanting to be physically close with you? You would probably take it personally and your self-esteem and feelings of worth could suffer. And it could also make you feel resentment towards your partner. Believe me when I tell you that you do not want your partner to resent you. Resentment has this nasty way of coming up over and over again during later conflicts.

In the end, I think it's essential that you and your mate realize that your sex life is going to change. And that it might not feel too good. And that the cause is sometimes completely out of your control. Prepare yourself for this change by talking about your expectations together. Come up with a strategy for bringing up issues created by the inevitable emotional and physical distance the two of you are about to experience. And promise to work really hard at (1) maintaining a sense of closeness when you cannot engage in intercourse and (2) reconnecting physically when you feel like you can.

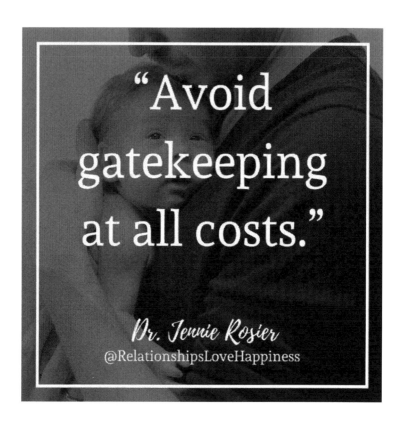

"Avoid gatekeeping at all costs."

Dr. Jennie Rosier

@RelationshipsLoveHappiness

Chapter Four:
The "You're Not Doing That Right" War

No, I'm not **still** talking about sex. Get your minds out of the gutter, people. What I'm talking about here is a situation where one parent (usually mom) takes control of the caregiving and then (either consciously or unconsciously) limit's dad's involvement by preventing him from caring for their child, criticizing how he cares for their child, or failing to encourage him. The mom in these situations acts as the "gatekeeper" of parenting knowledge. This is an extremely common dynamic that happens in many relationships after baby makes three. And if you don't nip it in the bud, it could continue for decades and the dreaded parent-child relationship (where one of you treats the other partner like a child) could develop.

Many times mom feels like dad is incapable of knowing what she knows and may begin to treat dad as beneath her. This makes sense- if you were a babysitter when you were younger, you probably have more experience around babies and young children than your man does. Young girls are more likely to be asked to watch smaller children (even if just for a few minutes here and a few minutes there) and are also more likely to play with dolls than young boys. Girls are also more likely to participate in activities as teenagers that involve young children— like babysitting, volunteering at a camp, working at a preschool, coaching a little kid sports team, etc. All of this combines to give women an edge when it comes to the amount of time they have caring for babies and young children. Go ahead- ask a group of young women and a group of young men if they have ever changed a diaper. Most of the women have and most of the men haven't. On top of all of this, women are typically (not always, clearly) the ones reading the parenting books, looking up online articles, and talking to their friends about parenting advice. All of this can cause women to feel like they know more about babies than their male partners; which can cause them to develop a bit of a superiority complex.

Okay. Some of you might be thinking- I've never changed a diaper! I've never babysat! I don't have any experience with babies! What the hell— I'm doomed! Breathe. You're fine. And, you'll *be* fine. In fact, I'd actually like to congratulate you for not spending your childhood consumed by following gender roles—good for you (and your parents)! You'll figure all of this baby stuff out. And if you have a partner, you'll figure it out *together*.

> The idea that some wives are the "gatekeepers" of the household, defining when and how husbands can get involved, constitutes a new perspective on how power issues may shape the negotiation of family work.
>
> (Allen & Hawkins, 1999)

Back to maternal gatekeeping. Like I said, there are three main ways that one can be a gatekeeper: (1) criticizing or mocking how dad cares for your child, (2) failing to encourage dad when he participates in caregiving, or (3) generally taking control of the care-giving and limiting dad's involvement by preventing him from caring for your child. I see women do this ALL OF THE TIME.

I'm sure you've heard a woman giggle while saying, "Make sure you hold the head, Honey" to her husband. Or maybe you've seen a Facebook post with a funny photo of a cute baby in a diaper that's on backwards and the caption, "Not sure if Matt will ever learn to diaper this baby. Lol!" Both of these examples are contemptuous ways to communicate that you know more about babies than your partner. To be clear, a handful of comments in the first year probably isn't going to cause much of a problem. But when this kind of maternal gatekeeping becomes part of your daily communication patterns, watch out! Not only can it be damaging to your relationship (making your partner feel emasculated and likely causing arguments), but it's also really difficult to break free from these destructive communication patterns once they've started and get back to a supportive and balanced communication climate.

Long-term maternal gatekeeping can easily manifest into criticism. Criticism is an ad hominem attack on someone's character. And we use criticism all of the time. "You never change his diaper! Why do I always have to do everything?!" You're not just complaining about your partner not changing the baby's diaper. You're taking it a step further and attacking the kind of person he is. "You never change his diaper" has some seriously nasty implications; especially when those words are coming from the person you love— the person who is with you on this amazing parenting journey. Individuals often make critical remarks out of pure desperation. You've been taking on more tasks, you feel like you're being taken advantage of, and then your partner doesn't do something that you wanted him to do or something that he said he would do and you criticize. I get it— it's frustrating and criticism is the go-to reaction for lots of people. Unfortunately, using criticism just adds fuel the fire that is the *You're Not Doing That Right War.*

Gatekeeping is often at the center of a downward spiral where you end up with a communication climate full of criticism

"Just by saying maternal gatekeeping exists doesn't mean all the responsibility should be on women to manage men. But it still serves as an impediment to the quality of the relationship between fathers and their children... and is part of the very complicated puzzle of how gender plays out in families."

–Sarah Schoppe-Sullivan, Ph.D.

and a relationship that doesn't feel that great to be in. Be aware of your communication tendencies, catch yourself before it's too late, and work hard to not let your frustration get the best of you.

In order to avoid criticism, you can learn to complain more effectively. Where complaints can sometimes be helpful (allowing people to take note and possibly make a change), criticisms tend to attack a person's disposition by blaming and generalizing the issue beyond the behavior in question. For instance, "I felt unsupported today when you kept not helping me when the baby was crying" is an example of a complaint; while "You never help me when the baby is crying" would be an example of criticism. Using words like "always" and "never" represent a critical remark.

I've narrowed complaining down to three steps. First, focus on **one** specific behavior when you're complaining to your mate. Second, don't overgeneralize the behavior being complained about to the person's personality. And third, avoid using absolutist language like "always" or "never" when describing human behavior (it's rarely a good idea). Something like, "It was really upsetting to me today when you said that you'd change his diaper and then you didn't. I had to stop what I was doing to get it done. It didn't feel fair." This complaint is specific, explained how you felt, and did not attack your mate's character.

Researchers agree with the idea that criticism tends to have negative outcomes. In fact, criticism has been linked to feelings of embarrassment[41] and lower relationship satisfaction[42] within the person being criticized. Furthermore, when comparing communication patterns of happy and unhappy couples, researchers have discovered that distressed couples tend to exhibit more negative verbal behaviors like sarcasm and criticism than happier couples.[43] Dr. John Gottman, one of my personal favorite marriage researchers, has even named criticism as one of his "Four Horsemen of the Apocalypse" when talking about the four signs which can reveal that couples are headed for break-up or divorce (defensiveness, contempt, and stonewalling being the other three).[44]

Another extremely common form of gatekeeping occurs when the woman (remember, I'm arguing in this chapter that women are usually the gatekeepers) fails to encourage dad when he participates in caregiving. I know, that kind of sounds like you have to baby him a little; which would be the opposite of what I've said so far, right? Encouraging your partner when he's doing something that he doesn't have much experience doing is different from talking down to your partner like he's a child.

Complimenting during this phase of life can be extremely helpful. Both men and women report that they highly value compliments in their romantic relationships.[45] Many researchers[46] have even claimed that complimenting can significantly add to the intimacy and relationship satisfaction that you experience with your partner. When your mate compliments you, you feel loved and valued, which can intensify the bond that the two of you share. Drs. Eve-Ann Doohan, Ph.D., and Valerie Manusov, Ph.D., of the University of Washington, have concluded that if you're satisfied with the complimenting that is occurring in your relationship, you're also more likely to be satisfied with your relationship as a whole.[47]

> Even after accounting for parents' beliefs about the father's role and the overall quality of the co-parenting relationship, greater maternal encouragement was associated with higher parent-reported father involvement. Additionally, low maternal criticism and high maternal encouragement shaped father involvement and increased parent relationship quality.
>
> (Schoppe-Sullivan, Brown, Cannon, Mangelsdorf, & Sokolowski, 2008)

Interestingly, research has shown that two-thirds of all compliments include the adjectives *nice, pretty, beautiful, good,* or *great,* and 90% of compliments include the verbs *like* or *love.*[48] Go against the grain and try to be more original by using other adjectives such as *lovely, outstanding, magnificent, gorgeous, amazing, delightful, superb, marvelous,* or *impressive* and other verbs like *admire, respect, enjoy,* or *adore.* Using these unique words will help your compliments stand out from the rest. Follow this set of complimenting "do's" and "don'ts" with the most important person in your life.

COMPLIMENTING DO'S AND DON'TS

DO use more unique adjectives & verbs in your tributes. DON'T forget about some of the more common terms. Sometimes speaking in an idiosyncratic way all of the time can cause people to view you as pompous.

DO compliment about specific things- "I really liked the way you handled the situation with our daughter. You were so calm, cool, and collected when she was crying forever." DON'T be so general that you're not personal- "You're great." Tell your partner why he or she is great.

DO act enthusiastic when complimenting. DON'T go overboard. This could make your accolades sound like sarcasm.

DO compliment about things your mate has chosen. DON'T always mention things your mate cannot change. So, instead of saying, "You have great eyes," you could say, "You're so patient when the baby cries." To become a patient dad, one generally has to put in a lot of effort. Complimenting someone on a skill is much better than complimenting someone on his or her physical beauty. Compliments about beauty should not be avoided completely; they just should not be the only type of compliment that you ever give your partner.

DO compliment daily. DON'T overdo it by complimenting about anything and everything. When you do this, your praises may seem less genuine.

DO compliment in front of others. DON'T compliment about personal or sensitive matters in front of others. For example, it would be completely inappropriate to praise your partner's love-making skills in front of your mom.

Effectively complimenting your mate is going to take some effort on your part. Pay attention to your partner interacting with your new, cute, little sack of potatoes and think of unique ways to compliment his efforts. Praise and support can empower him to learn more about caring for a baby, want to participate more in the caregiving, and inspire him to become in-tune with his new baby. Complimenting his behaviors, thanking him for his efforts, and reassuring him when he looks like he's struggling can help you get through the *You're Not Doing That Right War* **and** the *Who Does More War*. If your man feels confident in his parenting abilities, he is much more likely to pull most (if not all) of his weight when it comes to sharing tasks related to parenting. Thus, a little complimenting can go a long way.

A third common form of gatekeeping occurs when the gatekeeper (again, usually the woman) just takes over so that everything is done right or the way that the gatekeeper wants it to be done.

This seems like a great idea at first. I know the thought process all too well: "Since I typically have to do things over again anyways, I should just do it right the first time so it can be done. If I let him do it, he'll just fuck it up. Then I'll have to do it myself, so I'll just do it first." And then you just do it. You do the dishes or you get your baby diapered and dressed or you make the dinner before he has a chance to even think about it. And then as the tasks pile up, you bitch about doing it all. The *You're Not Doing That Right War* and the *Who Does More War* are deeply connected to each other. If you have that first war, you're probably going to experience the other.

I don't think that women gatekeep intentionally. And I would also argue that most women don't even realize that they're doing it. Regardless of why women do it, research has shown that the frequency of gatekeeping is a reflection of women more than men. Dr. Sarah Schoppe-Sullivan, a professor of human sciences and psychology at Ohio State University, has argued that "fathers' characteristics are less predictive of maternal gatekeeping than mothers' characteristics." Contrary to what I think many moms believe, it's not generally about the father's willingness to parent or about the father's actual parenting abilities. It's not even usually about the father's personality. Instead, a woman's likelihood to gatekeep is much more dependent on her own perceptions of parenthood, feelings about a man's role, acceptance of cultural pressure, and personal beliefs about men in general. For example, one study showed that the more sexist beliefs women hold about men, the more likely they are to gatekeep[49]. If a woman has traditional gender role expectations, she will be more likely to frequently gatekeep than if she has more progressive or equality-based expectations. Or, if a woman has personal beliefs that men are less-than or completely incapable of child-rearing or anything for that matter (you'd be surprised how many women believe they are superior to men), she will be more likely to frequently gatekeep.

Then there's the whole pressure that many women feel to be the *perfect mom* (whatever the fuck that means). We, both men and women, are inundated with messages about perfect motherhood all day long. It's really difficult to not let these messages impact our parenting belief systems. Television, movies, social media, and even going to the playground or mommy-and-me playgroups can leave a serious impression on our motherhood expectations. As Dr. Schoppe-Sullivan has said, "gatekeeping really seems to depend on how much a woman internalizes societal standards about being a good mom." The more you care about being perceived as one of those good or perfect moms (however you define it), the more likely you're going to struggle giving your partner any control in creating that image.

> Intensive mothering norms prescribe women to be perfect mothers. These norms have severe costs for women's family and work outcomes; including the increased likelihood for women to experience burnout.
>
> (Meeussen & Van Laar, 2018)

Maybe you don't feel like you have a strong global desire to be a perfect mother. But, I would bet that you're still heavily influenced by this idea when making decisions about some aspects of your parenting behaviors. For example, I consistently gatekeep when it comes to my children's clothing. I've always chosen my kids' clothes. I pick them out when buying them, I pick them out each morning, and when they're little, I even help them get clothes I've picked out onto their little bodies. I also wash all of the clothes in our family and I'm generally called upon when a piece of clothing is lost in the abyss that is our home. Everything about clothes falls in my domain.

I usually deal with clothes before my husband has a chance to even think about it and I've also been known to verbally stop him from completing this parenting chore: "Don't worry about it— I'll get their clothes." And while I sometimes bitch about the amount of work I've *willingly* taken on, I also <u>do</u> <u>not</u> want to let go of control here. In fact, the thought of allowing someone else to be in charge of clothing sometimes stresses me out. If I let the kids pick out their own clothes (which I've actually been working on), they might pick out something that looks ridiculous or has a stain or a rip. And then someone who they interact with during the day might think, "What the hell? Why are his clothes so dirty? Does his mother never wash them?" Clearly, that would be a terrible assumption made about ME! And even though I don't generally feel like I need to be a perfect mother, this assumption that *might* be made by a person who I *probably* don't even know would really bother me. And that is likely due to the expectations I've developed over decades of media exposure and cultural socialization about motherhood. Or let's imagine that I let my husband be in charge of buying clothing (That's never going to happen—LOL). Heaven forbid that there might not be enough socks in the stockpile one morning because my husband didn't pay attention to how quickly the kids were losing them. And then one day, my kids might not have ANY socks! And they'd have to JUST PUT THEIR SHOES ON! Oh, the agony! It sounds silly when I write it all out, but the feelings I have about needing to control this part of parenthood are real.

It's important to talk about this topic with your partner before you start a family and then promise to revisit it whenever one of you is feeling any tension related to gatekeeping. Be open with your mate about the typical amount of anxiety you have about perfection. If you know that you currently have control issues, understanding that this could easily get worse when baby arrives is important. And as I explained in the beginning of this book, talking about your expectations with each other early and often is really important.

In the end, try to avoid telling your partner how he should or should not care for his child. Bite your tongue. He may not have the same knowledge about newborns or children as you, but he's a grown-ass man who is perfectly capable of figuring it out. Make sure that he knows you support him and his efforts. Express your appreciation for everything that he does and compliment him. And lastly, work hard on not being so hard on yourself. Parenthood is not easy and perfection (or anything close to that) should never be a goal of any parent. Think critically about why you feel like you have to take over, adjust the expectations you've allowed the media and yourself to set for yourself, and work towards breathing, letting go, and welcoming imperfection. Avoiding gatekeeping will not only enable your baby daddy to be more involved, but it will also decrease conflict in your relationship.

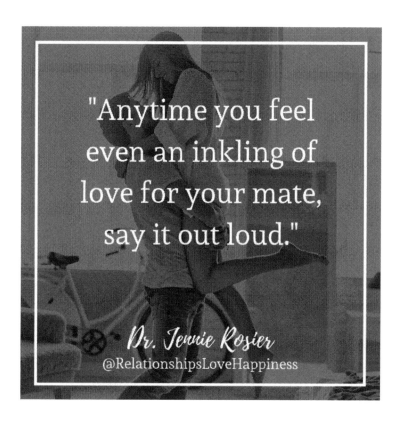

"Anytime you feel even an inkling of love for your mate, say it out loud."

Dr. Jennie Rosier
@RelationshipsLoveHappiness

Chapter Five:
The "There's No Time" War

Before children enter the picture, most people get to spend a significant amount of time with their partners and a significant amount of time by themselves. You want to go to the store? Go. You want to go out with your friends? Set it up. You want to eat dinner at your mom's house? Do it. Three date nights in one week? Spend. Your. Money.

> When interviewing couples where both partners work, researchers found that it is extremely common for husbands and wives to experience an initial decline in frequency of leisure activities during the first year of parenthood.
>
> (Claxton & Perry-Jenkins, 2008)

I don't know about you, but our pre-kids life was filled with going out to the movies, dinner dates, hanging out with friends, watching our favorite tv shows uninterrupted on our couch, vacations, snuggling under the covers on the weekends, making food together, parties, going shopping, having conversations with other humans, and WHATEVER ELSE WE WANTED TO DO (finances permitting, of course). We didn't have to check with anyone if we wanted to go somewhere. We didn't have to consider someone else's well-being or schedule when planning a vacation. We didn't get interrupted by tiny people who needed our immediate attention. And we sure as hell didn't have to worry about finding (and paying for) a babysitter when we wanted to go see the latest blockbuster movie... we just came up with the idea, got in the car, and went. Same with alone time. If I wanted to go somewhere by myself or if my husband wanted to go out with his friends, we just told each other and went. We had all of the time in the world (maybe not all of the money back then, but we had a lot of time).

Then, we had twins. And our time spent alone together and apart came to an end. An abrupt end. All of our couple time became family time. And all of our individual time became family time. Basically, all of our time was now family time.

Our twins were always with us. If we were together, our twins were there, too. In addition, they didn't go to daycare. One of us was always with them; 24/7. At the time, we lived in Indiana; which was a 12-hour drive from our family and friends in Maryland. Sure, we had some friends in Indiana, but the funny thing about this stage in your life is that lots of people you know are having babies at the same time that you're having babies. It's difficult to ask someone to watch your baby when they also have a baby; and we had TWO babies! It seemed impossible. Needless to say, date nights were not part of our weekly, monthly, or even yearly (!) routine anymore. And alone time seemed downright mean— "Can you watch the twins, who cry all of the time and rarely sleep, by yourself while I go get a pedicure?" So, we rarely did it.

If you're fortunate enough to live near family and friends who lovingly volunteer to care for your new baby, take them up on their offers. Probably not right away, but when you start to feel comfortable leaving your baby for an hour or two, let the kind people in your life who are willing to watch your precious little cherub actually watch your precious little cherub.

I have to admit; my husband and I weren't the best at this. Like I said, when we lived in Indiana, we didn't have many options. People definitely offered, but we would brush it off as them just being nice. I mean, who would *really* want to babysit *two* infants? We didn't take the baby-watching proposals seriously. Looking back, we probably should have.

What did we do to stay connected? We would put the twins down for a nap or for bed at night and then we would order some yummy food and watch a movie together. Or we would put our twins in their gigantic double stroller and take them for walks so we could talk about our days and our future plans while they were either entertained by the scenery or asleep from the movement. We lived for those walks and movie nights. We worked hard at having that focused time as often as possible; which ended up being about 2-3 times a week. It's actually not as difficult as you would think to find time to talk and connect when you have a baby. When kids get older and learn to talk (and learn to interrupt), finding a quiet time to have a conversation seems impossible sometimes. Trust me when I say that it just gets harder to find quality emotional connection time with your partner as your family expands and your children get older.

> Parenting can be stressful for couples as they find themselves with less time for adult activities that they may have enjoyed previously (e.g., dining out, theater).
>
> (Gillath, Karantzas, & Fraley, 2016)

We moved to Virginia when our twins were about 15 months old. We lived a lot closer to our family and friends and the babysitting offers started again. Unfortunately, we still were quite apprehensive. Our twins didn't know these family members very well and we weren't sure if anyone could handle our, many times, difficult-to-handle twin toddlers. Then we had another baby and the offers became few and far between. That's another funny thing about this time in your life. In our experience, people don't tend to offer to babysit more children than they had/have themselves. Both of our moms and most of our friends only had two children. The idea of watching three kids (two of which were twins) when you don't have a lot of experience watching three, well… it can be overwhelming. Then we had a fourth child. You can imagine what happened next.

But even then, we were both rather attached to our kids and we just weren't ready to leave them with anyone that often. On top of that, it seemed rude to ask someone to watch our four children without paying them. So, for a while, we relied on babysitters if we wanted a date night. This was *so* expensive and stressful to coordinate; causing us to only go on an actual date night 1-2 times a year.

Lucky for us, my mom moved to our same town when our youngest child was about 2.5 years old and she became a consistent figure in our children's lives. She was so incredibly helpful at getting us on a more frequent date night routine; increasing our outings by ourselves to about once a month! She even watched all four of them overnight several times (thanks, mom!). It was one of those situations where we didn't realize how badly we needed the date nights (or just uninterrupted conversation) until we started having them again regularly. It's been wonderful. And we've since worked diligently at trying to keep a regular date night schedule.

Interestingly, Drs. Amy Claxton and Maureen Perry-Jenkins discovered, in their 2008 study published in the *Journal of Marriage and Family*, that in dual-earning households, wives who reported spending more leisure time with their husbands before baby arrived also reported more marital love and less conflict during the first year of parenthood[50]. Experiencing the dramatic decrease in couple alone time didn't impact them as negatively if they experienced a lot of shared couple time before baby arrived. It's as if a buffer was created for the wives. When they experienced the inevitable decrease in the amount of one-on-one time, they were resilient. Maybe this is because during all of that quality alone time they had with their husbands, they talked about this expectation. Or maybe they even prepared for it. Or maybe it's just the idea that spending a lot of quality time together initially allows couples to "get through" this difficult lack of quality alone time.

Another finding from this study that I find fascinating is related to the husbands. Specifically, husbands who reported a lot of independent leisure time before baby arrived also reported less feelings of marital love and more instances of marital conflict during the first year of parenthood. So, if your husband goes out with his friends or does activities by himself a lot, the sudden shift from individual, many times self-care-focused, alone time to constant family time can be a major shock to their system.

Thus, the transition from a lot of individual alone time to constant family time is noticeably harder for men to cope with than the transition from a lot of couple time to constant family time is for women to cope with. This is important. Clearly, spending a significant amount of time together before baby arrives will not completely eliminate the conflict you could face related to the dramatic change in who you spend your time with, but it couldn't hurt, right? And maybe we need to be more cognizant of the fact that many (but not all) men really struggle with the sudden lack of alone time. Spending time together as a couple and being sensitive to a partner's struggles in this domain is definitely something you should give a shot. Just a thought.

Researchers studied 52 couples who became parents during their first year or second year of marriage. All of the couples in the study reported decreases in their feelings of love, marital satisfaction, and frequency of couple activities after having a baby.

(MacDermid, Huston, McHale, 1990)

You and your partner need to balance your own personal needs with the needs of your relationship and the needs of your child. You can't pour from an empty cup. Self-care and independent alone time are important to help you recharge. And you *both* need this time. For me, high quality independent time is getting a pedicure, going to bed early, grabbing lunch with a friend, attending one of those paint night events, and even grocery shopping alone (Ha!). On the other hand, my husband highly enjoys going for a long drive (in his Mustang Cobra— he's a car guy), walking around a car show talking to other car guys, or going for a run. Figuring out what brings you solace and what helps you de-stress is a vital first step to coping with the *There's No Time War*. Maybe it's working out, sleeping more, hiking, reading a good book with a cup of coffee, taking a bath, going to therapy, hanging out with your friends, eating healthy meals, playing video games, attending church, meditating, volunteering, or just going for a walk around the block.

Talk to each other about what you like to do independently. And talk about how much alone time you'd ideally like to have after the baby arrives. And then realize that you're each probably not going to get that much time. Make a realistic plan together. And promise to be flexible. Some days baby might really need Mom or might really need Dad and that plan that one of you had to go out with friends could get pushed back a few days or weeks. It's great to talk about expectations and make plans for the future, but it's even better to plan for being adaptable and willing to forgo some of your self-care and independent activities from time to time.

Consider thinking of new activities that can "count" as quality independent time for you. These ideas might not come to you until you actually have children. For example, if you would have told me that grocery shopping alone would bring me great pleasure 15 years ago, I would have laughed. But now, I seriously LIVE for those shopping trips where I can slowly walk up and down the aisles, carefully pick out produce, think about new recipes, and even price check products against each other without having to deal with a tantrum about buying (or not buying) something, a strict timeline, or a small person asking me 294 questions. It's an incredible experience that only a parent can truly appreciate. I feel refreshed, accomplished, and centered when I get to grocery shop alone. It is glorious[b].

Be cognizant of the things that make you feel this way after you have a baby and engage in those activities along with some of your favorite pre-baby independent activities.

You also need to attend to the needs of your romantic relationship. Talk about your favorite couple activities, realize that you might not be able to do those exact activities as frequently as you would like after baby arrives, and then try to come up with new ways to connect and spend time together. You're going to have to get creative since you're about to have another human's needs to take into consideration. For example, when our twins were four and our third child was one, we would put them all down for the night, grab the baby monitor, turn off our phones, pour a couple glasses of

---

[b] Yes, Marti. I still think of you every single time I say *glorious*. That one's for you.

wine, and sit on our front porch together. This was our way of connecting. We had uninterrupted conversations and just relaxed together. Sometimes, we would spice it up by playing cards or reading a book together. We did this at least once a week. It was a wonderful time that we both looked forward to.

Every couple is different though, and every relationship has different needs. Communicate what you think you'll want and need to your partner. And listen to your partner's physical and emotional connection needs. Some couples need more together time to feel fulfilled and others are okay with less. Figuring this out is vital to surviving this war.

Many people are not okay with leaving their baby with someone. I get it. I was one of those people. Even if you don't want to separate from your baby, I think it's still really important to go out with your baby in tow. Believe me when I say that small babies are actually quite easy to take with you on a date. Take advantage of this time (when you can strap your baby to your body and go pick apples/eat dinner/take a romantic walk with your partner). It's easy to tote your little one around with you when they're babies. It just gets harder the older they get and the more children you add to your tribe.

When our fourth child, Rex, was 2 months old, we got a sitter for our older three children and we signed up for a food tour in our little downtown culinary district. It was soooo fun. We got to eat, walk, drink, hear some fun historical facts about our city, and have a conversation with each other; all while our new baby slept. It was really exciting for us to try new food at new restaurants we hadn't been to before. Taking a sleeping baby out with you on dates doesn't last very long. Babies start to stay awake for longer periods of time as they get older and this makes it more difficult to bring them along.

When your baby gets a little older, you might not want to take them with you on dates anymore, but you might not be ready to leave them either. You're going to have to get even more creative when trying to find emotional connection time. Maybe you make sure that you talk on the phone with each other on your lunch breaks each day or while driving to and from work. Or maybe you promise to have quality conversations and snuggle time when baby is asleep.

Once you actually start to feel more comfortable leaving your baby with someone (expect that this could take weeks, months, or even years for some people), take a break and have a date where you can seriously connect. Then make a semi-consistent plan to continue to reconnect. And contemplate adding some new, exciting, and interesting date night activities into your rotation. It's important to spice things up from time to time.

While it may be obvious to most of you, engaging in novel, amusing, and exciting activities with your partner is **very** beneficial to your relationship. Some of us can get bored with the monotony of day-to-day life. When you have children, the schedules and extra tasks and routines can easily take over and make your previous life seem spontaneous and impulsive (regardless of how it actually was) compared to what you're currently dealing with. Spicing things up with a little excitement here and there is usually an easy fix for these feelings.

> "Nobody is too busy. It's just a matter of priorities. Make your marriage a priority."
>
> –Meygan Caston,
> Creator, Marriage 365

Dr. Arthur Aron, Ph.D., of the State University of New York at Stony Brook, and several of his colleagues[51] conducted five studies to thoroughly examine how participating in activities with your partner influences the quality of your relationship.

Studies one and two found a strong positive relationship between participating in new and exciting activities and experienced relationship quality. So, as the activities in your relationship increase in perceived newness and excitement, your experienced relationship quality also tends to increase.

These first two studies were correlational in nature (i.e. the studies showed that the two variables were related, but they did not show which variable caused the other—does increased relationship quality cause people to engage in more exciting activities OR does engaging in more exciting activities cause increased relationship quality?). Because of this, the researchers decided to conduct three more studies to help shed some light on the cause-effect relationship between these two variables.

The next three studies examined (in a few different ways) the impact that engaging in exciting and not-so-exciting activities has on experienced relationship quality with dating and married couples. All of the studies had couples come to a lab and complete relationship quality surveys prior to engaging in a predetermined activity and then taking the same set of relationship quality surveys.

The researchers discovered that shared participation in novel and arousing activities, compared with shared participation in mundane activities, increased experienced relationship quality. Interestingly, participants' experienced relationship quality significantly increased after only about 10 minutes of engaging in the new and interesting activity! The take-home message: take an hour or so to plan a few fun, interesting activities with your partner to enhance your relationship quality.

I would venture to say that a lack of excitement, as opposed to a lack of stability, is likely the more common relationship problem; especially when kids and routines and deadlines and more work and crying are thrown into the mix. Whether you've been together for 6 months or for 40 years, spending new and exciting quality time with your partner can help build and maintain your relationship at any stage.

Having trouble thinking of date ideas? Here are 10 often inexpensive date ideas that you can do with or without your baby tagging along.

10 DATE IDEAS

Find your way through a corn maze; which is a fun way to see how well you work together as a team.

Get scared together at a local haunted house or other haunted attraction (like a haunted forest). You could end the night with a scary movie cuddled up together.

Pick out pumpkins and carve them at home while sharing your favorite childhood Halloween memories with each other.

Go for a walk around the neighborhood. Hold hands, walk around, notice the world around you, and talk. Believe me when I say that talking with your partner is one of the best ways to maintain your relationship.

Take a class together- you could learn how to make pottery, cook a delicious meal, bake something yummy, play a sport, make a model airplane or car, paint, or even learn a second language together!

Get bundled up in your cutest snow gear, buy some inner tubes, and spend the day flying down a steep hill with your partner. Better yet, if you live within driving distance of a ski resort that offers tubing as an option, go there.

Snuggle up on the couch and watch your favorite romantic movie.

Strawberries and apples and peaches... oh my! Find a U-Pick orchard near you and spend the day perusing the land for the best produce money can buy.

Rent a boat. Whether you go paddle-boating or speedboating, spending the day on a boat in the middle of a lake, river, bay, or ocean is an extremely romantic date where you can get away from it all with your partner. Look up local bodies of water near you and you'll likely find some kind of boat rental nearby. Pack a meal for an added romantic touch.

Search for stars. Choose some constellations to find, print out information about each constellation, get a blanket, and lay out under the stars.

I know what you're probably thinking: "How can life **always** be new and exciting?" It doesn't have to be. Instead, spicing up your relationship by doing something new every once in a while is a really great thing. Just switching around your daily routine can keep things interesting. Take up a new hobby together, go on vacation, or just change out your regular date night restaurant for an interactive dining experience like a Japanese steakhouse or fondue restaurant. It will be a new experience, and if you've ever been to one of those restaurants before you know that they're definitely exciting.

As your children age, at least for me and my marriage, quality couple time continues to be extremely important. You cannot let your children completely consume your life. You have to work hard at continuing to maintain your relationship with the person you created this wonderful life with.

Emotional connection is at the foundation of every good relationship. It's vital that you continue to nurture your bond by learning more about one another, inviting each other to self-disclose and talk about your days, emotionally supporting one another through stressful times, and discussing decisions that impact your family together (instead of on your own). You need to work towards being in-tune with one another. Being in-tune with how our partners feel and helping them in times of distress, standing by them

"Emotional intimacy is ultimately the glue that holds a relationship together, after the initial excitement fizzles. Couples who are emotionally intimate can overcome conflict more easily because they understand each other better and are able to communicate their feelings to each other."

–Caleb Backe,
Health & Wellness Coach
Maple Holistics

in times of decision, and playing on their team while trying to navigate this crazy thing called parenthood can easily enhance feelings of closeness, intimacy, and satisfaction in your relationship. The only way that you can build and maintain this emotional connection is to spend quality, conversation-having time together.

Overall, you and your partner need to work hard at carving out quality couple time and enough independent alone time in your ridiculously busy new life so that you are both satisfied. But maybe even more important, you both need to learn to appreciate the new family time. Recognize that this is what you've always wanted—having a family, spending your days together, laughing with each other, and working as a team to build a future that you'll be proud of. Acknowledge your thankfulness and express your gratitude often.

"Just so you know, most of us are winging it, too."

Dr. Jennie Rosier
@RelationshipsLoveHappiness

Chapter Six:
The "What Are We Going to Do with Them" War

It was the end of a long day. It had snowed since the wee hours of the morning and around 5am, we got a text message that said schools were closed. Since my job is more flexible, I cancelled my classes for the day and stayed home with our four children. My husband left for work at 6:45am and the kids were beaming with snow day excitement. We watched a movie and they played with their toys until they wore me down with all of their begging to go outside.

Around 9am, they put on two full layers of clothes, zipped up their snow suits, buttoned up their jackets, and put on their hats and gloves. They played outside for 10 peaceful minutes before our littlest came running in scream-crying about his older brother throwing a snowball directly in his face and hurting him. I called his brother inside only to hear him yell, "I didn't do anything to that BABY! He's such a baby! I'm not coming in; I just got out here!" I decided to ignore the older brother (it's important to pick my battles, right?), comforted the younger brother, and sent my little one back outside.

About 15 minutes later, they were all back inside removing their soaking wet clothes onto the kitchen floor. And then the whining started: "Can we have hot chocolate?!!!" "I'm SOOOOO cold!!" "Get me some clothes, Mom!" "Paxton was mean to me outside!" "I was not mean to anyone!" The whining and complaining lasted the entire time I made them grilled cheese and hot chocolate. Once I got them all to sit and put food on the table, I was already quite worn down. It was 9:45am.

The day was far from over. I put a movie on the television and gave each child a blanket and a bowl of popcorn. I left the family room to try to decompress. No less than 10 minutes into the movie I hear a THUD, followed by a SCREAM. It was our four-year-old, Rex. I ran into the family room and yelled: "What's happening?!

Aren't y'all watching a movie?! I can't even have 10 minutes of peace without one of y'all hurting someone?!" Meanwhile, Rex is screaming that Vivian pinched him when he refused to move over on the couch and that it "Hurt weally, weally bad!" and that he fell off the couch when trying to come tell me about the pinch. It was 10:15am.

The rest of our day was filled with sibling arguments, a child breaking one of my favorite coffee mugs, a few more sibling-induced injuries, someone squeezing a full tube of toothpaste out onto the bathroom counter, and a whole lot of yelling (from all five of us). But there wasn't a ton of punishment. I threatened that I would take a privilege away but never followed through. I said that they would lose a toy they were fighting over, but never actually took the toy. I even said that I was disappointed in their argumentativeness, but I didn't model much positive behavior for them. By the end of the day, I was completely drained, and I couldn't wait for my husband to get home.

He arrived home as I was putting dinner (that I made) on the table while listening to two of our children make audible vomit noises; complaining that the food was "DIS-GUS-TING!"

While we were all eating, Gavin and Paxton started bickering about who knows what. And then one of them said, "You wanna go, bro?!" Before I knew it, they were both on the floor wrestling around screaming about some bullshit problem. My husband picked up one of the boys and told him that he had to sit on the steps until he calmed down. The other one was sent to a nearby bench. They sat there. They didn't complain and they didn't get up. Then my freaking husband looked at me and said, "What the hell, Jennie?! Why are they on the verge of killing each other?! What did you do with them all day?!"

I loudly replied, "Excuse me?!"

This was when the *Who Does More War* and the *What are We Going to Do with Them War* were officially in full swing. We continued to ~~calmly discuss~~ yell at each other about it all:

"Why don't you follow through?!"
"We've all been cramped in the house most of the day. Tensions are high."
"You need to control them better!"
"I was here all day by myself with them! Sometimes, it's not worth the fight."
"You have to follow through! They're just going to walk all over you."

When you argue with your partner, especially about discipline, you run the risk of increasing relationship dissatisfaction, lowering your ability to solve the issue, and even causing your children to begin to think that they could use your relationship discord as leverage against you and/or your partner in the future. Further, Dr. E. Mark Cummings, a developmental psychology professor and researcher at the University of Notre Dame, has found in dozens of studies that children who are privy to destructive conflict between their parents can become distraught, worried, hopeless, and anxious.[52]

> "Disagreements about discipline can easily lead to marital problems."
>
> –Amy Morin, LCSW
> Author, "13 Things Mentally Strong People Don't Do"

In my experience (and the experience of thousands of parents who have participated in academic research for the past several decades in this field of study), there are a few things exacerbating the frequency and intensity of this war—one or both parents (1) disagreeing about how to discipline their kids, (2) taking on good cop/bad cop roles and not being happy about the role they took on or were given, (3) not being able to fulfill the discipline plans previously agreed upon, (4) being hypocritical when disciplining or talking to partner about discipline, and (5) comparing your kids to other people's kids.

Children can be rambunctious, inconsiderate, loud, destructive, unpredictable, and if they're anything like my four, they can also be downright rude at times. They also have big emotions without much ability to effectively cope with them. These factors coupled with the idea that what works with one child might not work with another child make disciplining children an often stressful and contentious task for parents.

This is why before kids enter the picture, it's so important to talk about discipline. This doesn't mean that having a conversation will necessarily stifle all conflict in this domain. But opening the lines of communication about this difficult subject matter can help the two of you when you get to the inevitable discipline obstacles you'll face as a couple.

Remember that you and your partner are two completely different people with completely different backgrounds, upbringings, and expectations that impact how you think parents should interact with, control, punish, and respect their children. Regardless of whether we liked or hated the way that our parents raised us, many individuals tend to adopt some or all of their parents' discipline strategies when parenting their own children. I've heard so many people say over the years, "My mom/dad used to do X, Y, and Z and I turned out okay." Because of how deeply ingrained many of our discipline values are and the strong inclination that many of us have to copy our parents, many people can be quite inflexible with their discipline plans; especially when they're confronted with any ideas that conflict with their own. Clearly, this can cause conflict in your marriage. Let's dive a little deeper into each of the main issues that intensify the *What are We Going to Do with Them War.*

When and How to Discipline

Parents often argue about which behaviors warrant discipline and how to actually go about executing discipline. You might think that an unfavorable behavior your child does is a big deal while your partner sees it as trivial and not worthy of a parental response. Or, you might both think that a punishment is needed, but disagree on what the punishment should be.

For example, I strongly believe that if our elementary-school age children get in trouble at school (it can't be that bad in elementary school, right?), they shouldn't also get in trouble (whatever that means) at home. A simple, "I'm sorry that happened today. Do you know now what you were expected to do?" is fine for me. And it's also fine for my husband. Well, now it is, but only after a long discussion we had about it.

The first time Gavin was sent to the principal's office, my husband was not on board with my idea. He insisted that we had to take away a privilege or ground him or something. And I insisted that Gavin had already gotten into enough trouble at school and that he had paid his dues. If I remember right, we settled on a super long discussion with Gavin about appropriate behavior at school (you know, one of those conversations that any 6-year-old would absolutely hate) and a time-out to think about how he could have behaved.

> The top 8 areas of concern for parents are generally related to food, phone/screen addiction, arguments, disrespecting elders, cleanliness, laziness, nagging, and stubbornness.
>
> (Biswal, Pathak, & Mishra, 2019)

A couple of weeks later, Gavin was in "trouble" at school again (I put trouble in quotes because the incidents that he was being reprimanded for were insignificant at best—for instance, one time Gavin got in trouble for jumping in line after a teacher had instructed him to stop jumping. So ridiculous, right? I thought so.). This time, my husband and I had the opportunity to talk about it together before we interacted with Gavin. Our thought process was something like this: "Well, the school seems rather strict. Clearly. He's getting called to the principle for jumping. And since he's not doing anything that severe and he's getting reprimanded at school. I guess we can just have a short discussion with him when he gets home."

We still have that rule today—if you get in trouble at school, you pay your dues there and you won't get in trouble again at home. And our kids know the rule; which you might think that knowing the rule would cause them to be purposefully disobedient at school, but it actually hasn't. They don't want to get called out by a teacher for doing something they shouldn't be doing and they definitely don't want to get sent to the principal's office. It's very embarrassing to them. What it has done is lower the insane amount of anxiety they felt when they got in trouble at school because they were worried about how we would react.

So, while my husband used to think that school issues needed to be punished and I didn't, we now both see the importance of our children not having stomach aches for the remainder of the school day as they wait for our potential reaction when they get home.

I think it's important to note that discussions about discipline don't always have a happy ending full of compromise and agreement. And most of the time, couples are arguing about more serious discipline tactics than whether a child gets a time out at home after being sent to the office at school. For example, your partner might be completely against spanking and you think that a certain amount and kind of spanking is totally acceptable for children. Or one of you might believe in using guilt while the other person believes that guilt trips are wrong and should be avoided. Or one of you might be completely against using time-outs as a discipline strategy while the other person thinks they're useful in certain situations. Still, there are other couples where one person doesn't believe in any form of discipline or punishment and the other person does. All of these instances involve difficult differences that can quickly turn into really tough conversations. One of you will need to concede a bit or even fully change their mind to remain united as a couple.

Couples additionally tend to argue about different ideas they have regarding age-appropriate discipline. For example, some people think that kids under 2 years of age need discipline and others believe that kids need to be a bit older before *any* discipline tactics are used. Or some people might believe that time-outs are best for toddlers and preschoolers, while others believe that time-outs should be reserved for elementary-school aged children.

All of these beliefs we have about punishment and discipline are rather deep-seated. We've developed them over decades of life experience with our own families, the media, and our culture. This can make it very difficult for us to be open to new ideas and especially difficult for our minds to actually be changed.

Fortunately, I'm not here to tell you which punishments are right or wrong or even if punishment as a whole is right or wrong. Sorry! Instead, like the rest of this book, my purpose is to make you aware of all of the things related to this issue that can cause serious problems in your relationship so that you can hopefully prepare for them. And in the next chapter, I'll provide you with tons of tips and tricks for actually starting and finishing these conversations.

> There are typically four main types of disciplining behavior used by parents: positive discipline, supervision, penalty, and aggressive discipline.
>
> (Koentjana, Abidin, Purboningsih, & Elsari, 2016)

Getting on the same page about what constitutes unacceptable behavior, what discipline looks like, and how you would ideally administer discipline are extremely messy, but absolutely necessary, topics to discuss with your partner.

Good Cop, Bad Cop Disagreements

We've all heard "good cop, bad cop" labels applied to parents in the real world and in the media. "Good cops" are typically described as parents who are permissive, soft, and fun-loving friends, while parents who take on the "bad cop" role tend to be more of a boring, strict disciplinarian. In some households, the roles are clear and rigid; with one parent almost always being the good cop and the other parent almost always being the bad cop. Other families, however, have parents who take on different roles based on the child and/or behavior being disciplined—imagine dad being a bad cop when it comes to disciplining his sons and a good cop when disciplining his daughters or a mom being a good cop when it comes to most issues, but a bad cop when it comes to her teens doing drugs or alcohol.

Good cop, bad cop parenting can often send mixed messages to children and is seen by some researchers[53] as an ineffective (and potentially damaging) parenting style. But alas, I'm not here to tell you about *how* to best discipline children. Back to the *What are We Going to Do With Them War*.

The part of good cop, bad cop parenting that can cause problems in your relationship is when one or both of you are not happy about the role you took on or ended up with by process of elimination. It's not fun being either of these roles all of the time. For example, the good cop might struggle to be taken seriously by their children and the bad cop might struggle to let loose and have fun with their kids. Resentment can build up if the unhappiness or discomfort with your role lasts too long.

> "Frequently, one parent wishes a softer approach, such as explaining, talking, and encouraging. The other parent wants to use a more stern style with harsher consequences."
>
> –Barbra Russell, *LPC*

Keeping the lines of communication open about this, oftentimes unconscious and dissonance-creating, decision to be the good cop or the bad cop is vital to avoiding resentment. Talk to your partner about which role you think you would like or brainstorm ideas about parenting styles you'd like to do instead of playing good cop, bad cop. And as usual, promise to be willing to openly and frequently talk about any dissatisfaction you might experience during those first couple of decades after your little disobedient and boundary-pushing bundle of joy arrives.

Discipline Plan Fulfillment

Let's imagine that you've talked and talked and talked with your partner about discipline and you've actually agreed on a clear, specific, solid discipline plan. You're both really happy with it and you're ready.

And then your baby turns into a preschooler and all hell breaks loose. She starts pitching epic fits in the aisles of your favorite grocery store that you can no longer go to out of pure embarrassment. She says "No!" to you on an hourly basis about the simplest parental requests. And she bites her friends whenever she's frustrated or just whenever she feels in the mood to inflict pain on another human.

Disciplining your child has now become a full-time job. Maybe your original plan doesn't seem right anymore. Or maybe you're just exhausted from disciplining non-stop. Whatever the reason, carrying out some elaborate (or maybe not-so-elaborate) discipline plan can seem overwhelming at best. Been there, felt that.

I'm the first person to admit that this whole parenting gig is incredibly difficult. It's complicated and trying and grueling. You're constantly questioning your decisions and wondering if you should try something else. And no matter how much you want to do something (i.e. discipline a certain way), it can be difficult to follow through every single time.

Our son Gavin has frequently tested our ability to follow through. Not so much because we were unsure about our discipline choices, but more because he was extremely mischievous as a young kid, he had really good excuses at times that were difficult to contest, and the frequency of these occurrences wore us down. Just to give you a small taste: Gavin once carved his name into the wood floor of our rental, filled a toilet to-the-brim with sand, poured a cup of water on each person's mattress about an hour before bedtime, broke a new-ish end table by standing on and then jumping off of it, wrote on the walls frequently and one time on our couch with permanent marker, and vacuumed up dog poop; ruining the vacuum cleaner forever. Oh yeah, he's also the kid I mentioned in the beginning of this book who peed in our washing machine. And just like the washing machine debacle, his reasoning for most of his behaviors has been that he was unaware that he couldn't do it. Another popular excuse is that he wanted to see what would happen. How can you argue with that? Gavin is a very literal child. If we never told him that something was off limits, how would he know?! And if he was just experimenting, how could we truly be angry?! He's definitely made us question our reactions over the years. He's also caused us to not follow through with whatever discipline strategy we had in place. And if one of us wanted to follow through and the other person didn't, conflict ensued.

The point is that every child is different and sometimes discipline plans need to change. Problems arise, however, when the two of you disagree on the alteration.

Hypocritical Partners

Another factor that I believe strongly impacts relationship conflict about discipline is when one or both parents are being hypocritical. Maybe you talk a lot about the negative outcomes of spanking, expect your partner to avoid the behavior, and then one day you find yourself hitting your child in anger. Or you say that you're adamantly against shame, expect your mate to avoid communicating in that way, and then during an argument with your ten-year-old, you yell, "You're such a bad kid! How could you have ever thought this behavior was okay?!" Clearly, these are problematic parenting experiences, but when your partner is privy to these interactions, you could be additionally creating problems in your relationship.

When one partner has expectations of the other that they fail to apply themselves, feelings of unfairness develop. Your mate might begin to feel like there is a double standard, "He always says that I shouldn't shame our children and yells at me when I slip up, but now he's shaming our child?!" This could cause serious issues in your relationship.

Unfortunately, I fall victim to this problem more often than I would like. For example, I regularly PREACH to my husband (and to parents at parenting workshops, students in my classes, interviewers in media appearances, and anyone who will listen to me, really) about not criticizing children. In fact, I talk about avoiding criticism in all relationships; oftentimes citing research that has revealed links between criticism and feelings of self-hatred, low self-esteem, hostility, and depression. AND THEN I CRITICIZE MY OWN PRECIOUS CHILDREN; which almost always starts an argument with my husband; first about my unacceptable actions and then second about how I expect him to avoid criticism and I cannot listen to my own sermon.

Unhealthy Comparisons

The last piece to the *What are We Going to Do with Them War* puzzle involves comparing your own children to other people's children. This is so dangerous and it can actually cause a great deal of blame, criticism, and general conflict within your romantic relationship.

I remember one of the first times we went on a multiple family vacation for a few nights. There were eight adults and lots of children; three were ours and there were about five or six more from the other three couples. It was the summer my husband and I were talking about maybe trying for a fourth child. I remember that because at one point during our argument about our children's annoying behavior I yelled, "They're all going to think we're insane when we tell them we willingly created yet another crazy, out-of-control child!" You see, our three children were not on their best behavior that vacation. And they were deliberately disobeying things that we said. In front of our friends. And their well-behaved children. It was as if our kids had decided that they were going to compete with each other for the Most Hellacious Child award. The more they misbehaved, the more we lost our cool, which caused them to act out, which made us yell more, which made them cry more. It was a vicious cycle and it was tough for us to deal with it all. Then, we turned on each other:

"Why didn't you stop him?!"
"You encouraged that behavior!"
"We look like idiots!"
"No one else's kid is acting like this!"
"You've lost control, and it shows!"

Looking back, it was such a silly argument. Our kids were just being kids. There were lots of people in the house, it was exciting, and they were acting crazy because the situation was crazy. Why wasn't anyone else's kid acting up? Who knows. But none of that actually matters. All children act out. Some do it in front of other people and some do it behind closed doors. No child (or adult) is perfect all of the time; or even most of the time.

Comparing your children to other people's children is a useless exercise. And fighting about it with your partner is pointless. No two children are alike. Some kids have moody days more often than others. Some kids are more comfortable than others at openly expressing their emotions. And some kids keep it together all day only to break down at bedtime. Every night. There's always going to be a child who cries less than your child, who sleeps longer than your child, who laughs and giggles more than your child, who is more polite than your child, who is calmer than your child, and who is… you get the point.

Loving your children for who they are and avoiding comparison is key to preventing this aspect of the *What Are We Going to Do with Them War*.

So, what can you do to prepare for this war? A great first step is to talk to your partner about certain discipline tactics (spanking, time-out, rational explanations, natural consequences, privilege elimination, etc.) that were used with each of you by your own parents. What were your evaluations of these tactics? Did you appreciate the discipline, learn something from it, and/or feel like it was traumatic? Hopefully, this initial discussion will begin to give you an idea about what sorts of discipline you and your mate might want to use with your own children. Talk about tactics you think are valuable and ones you are completely against. And then go to the back of this book where I have so many more discussion questions to help you figure out this whole discipline thing. Lastly, it never hurts to read more about the discipline strategies you've decided on. And as always, be ready to adapt your discipline plan with each new child and/or if something from your plan is not working.

"Love is like a plant. You need to nurture it. You need to continuously work to maintain it and make it better. You can't just put it in the cupboard."

John Lennon

Dr. Jennie Rosier
@RelationshipsLoveHappiness

Chapter Seven:
Talking It Out with 75 Conversation-Starters

Okay, so you've been reading about typical post-baby conflict for the last five chapters and you've probably developed some new realistic expectations about what parenthood is going to do to your relationship. You've even probably had a few conversations with your partner about chores, sex, gatekeeping, time, and discipline while reading this book. And hopefully, you've started thinking about how you and/or your partner might cope with these issues.

In order to help you feel more prepared, I've included a few dozen conversation-starting questions in this chapter about the five common conflicts. Anytime you and your partner have some time (over dinner, while you're driving together in the car, on your lunch break, before bed, etc.), tackle a few of these questions together. And since simply having conversations isn't always enough, I'll also help you create a shared parenting vision in chapter ten.

The Who Does More War

1. From what you remember, how did your own parents divide chores when you were a child? What was your perception of that division? What parts of your parent's division of labor would you like to model and what would you like to change when thinking about dividing labor in your own relationship?

2. What gender role expectations do you have about chores? Do you have more traditional ideas about household tasks or more progressive ideas? (Remember: there is no right or wrong idea here— you just need to agree to keep the peace) What would you like to be in charge of and what do you absolutely hate doing?

3. Do you or your partner plan to breastfeed? If yes, what equally time-consuming chores (maybe diapers?) could the other partner work hard at taking over? If no, how would you like to divide up the formula feeding (i.e. one person mixes and feeds and the other

person washes bottles or you both do both or one of you will take over feeding while the other person does some other chores)?

4. How are you going to combat the lack of sleep that new babies bring? Will one of you be taking the night shift alone or will you be taking turns (if your baby is breastfed, mom will need to pump enough milk during the day to cover dad's turn)?

5. Who is going to be in charge of food? Buying groceries, planning meals, preparing them, and packing lunches and snacks when you go out?

6. If you have other children already, how would you like to divvy up caring for them *and* the new baby?

7. How are you planning to deal with the influx of appointments? Who is going to make the doctor appointments and who is going to go to them?

8. How do you each deal with stressful situations? How do you think your ability (or lack of ability) to deal with stress will impact how you care for your crying baby and your emotionally unstable toddler?

9. How much maternity and paternity leave do you each get from work? How can you best utilize this time off so that it best benefits your family?

10. What family and friends are willing to help you with the transition during the first few days/weeks? Do you have family and friends you could ask to make you food or come over to give you a break for a shower?

11. How are you going to address childcare? Do you plan to be a stay-at-home parent and care for your baby yourself? Or will you need childcare after your maternity and paternity leaves end? Have you thought about what kind of childcare you're interested in (daycare center, in-home childcare center, in-home nanny, a trusted family member, etc.)? What can the two of you afford in your town/city?

12. If both of you work, which of your jobs is more flexible? Who is going to take off when your baby gets sick? Or when the weather closes your child's school?

13. Who will take your baby to and from daycare each day? How will you split up the driving when extracurricular activities begin?

14. Speaking of extracurriculars, how important are they to you? Do you see them as a waste of time (and/or money), valuable, or vital to your future child's life experience?

15. Will you limit the number of activities your child participates in? What kinds of boundaries do you think children should have when it comes to extracurriculars? Are there specific ages where you think extracurriculars are more important? Are there certain activities you would really like your child to participate in or avoid?

The Why Don't You Want to BLEEP Me Anymore War

16. What do you find most attractive about your partner?

17. What does your partner do for you that makes you feel most loved? What does your partner do that makes you feel sexy?

18. What do you wish your partner did for you to make you feel loved? What do you wish your partner did to make you feel sexy?

19. What do you love hearing your partner say to you?

20. What do you wish your partner said to you?

21. How important is physical touch to you? What kinds of physical touch do you like the most? The least?

22. How important is an active and satisfying sex life to you? Be honest.

23. How do you expect your sex life will change after baby arrives? What are your expectations for your sex life three months after your baby is born? At the six-month mark? What do you expect your sexual relationship to look like when you have a toddler or preschooler?

24. How do you plan to deal with the dramatic decrease in sexual contact after baby arrives? What can each of you do to help the other person still feel desired even if you can't engage in intercourse? What are some ways you can connect physically and emotionally to fill the sexual contact void?

25. If you plan to co-sleep with your baby, where could you have sex if baby is in your bed? You might have to get creative if co-sleeping is in your parenting plan. Just don't let "but the baby is in the bed" become an excuse for not having sex.

26. How will you carve out time for intimacy? What do you promise to do to keep those feelings of sexual connection strong?

27. What are your thoughts on scheduling sex? What do you think are the disadvantages of creating a schedule? How do you think scheduling sex could be beneficial?

28. What kind of schedule would be ideal for each of you? How can you meet in the middle to make everyone happy?

29. How does sexual rejection make you feel? What can both of you do to cope with one of you not being interested in sex as much as they once were?

30. How can you talk about sexual issues in the future so that you don't hurt one another's feelings?

The You're Not Doing That Right War

31. What kind of experience do you have caring for babies and small children? How do you think your experience, or lack of experience, with babies and children will impact how you care for your own child?

32. Who's parenting skills do you admire? These could be your own parents, people in the media, or other couples/individuals you know. What do these people do that you respect?

33. What aspects of parenting do you wish you knew more about?

34. What aspects of parenting intimidate you? What parts are you nervous about or cause you anxiety?

35. How can you gently tell your partner that you don't like or approve of the way they are caring for your child? How can you promise to bring up this subject without offending one another? How would you like to be approached about this topic?

36. Some people value encouragement more than others. How much of a role does encouragement play in your ability to feel worthy and good about your actions?

37. What is one of the best compliments your partner has said to you in the past?

38. What kinds of compliments do you wish your partner would give you more often?

39. How much do you think about being the "perfect mom" or "perfect dad"? How do you think this will impact your parenting choices?

40. How can you each work towards welcoming imperfection?

The There's No Time War

41. How satisfied are you with the time you currently get to spend with your partner? What do you wish would change about your current time spent together?

42. What does your ideal date look like? What kinds of dates do you like the most?

43. What has been your favorite date up to this point?

44. What kind of dates do you wish the two of you did more of? What's your dream date?

45. How do you decompress together after a long day?

46. What is your favorite activity to go do without your partner?

47. How often do you get to visit with your friends? How satisfied are you with the amount of time you get with your friends?

48. How often do you get to visit with your family? How satisfied are you with the amount of time you get with your family?

49. How often do you get to do something for yourself (i.e. self-care)? How satisfied are you with the amount of self-care time you get?

50. What kinds of self-care activities bring you the most peace and/or happiness?

51. How important is independent time to you? How much do you feel like you need to feel fulfilled?

52. What do you think happens after a baby is born regarding time? What is your expectation about how your time with family, friends, each other, and yourself is going to change after children enter the picture?

53. How are you going to cope with the drastic lack of friend, family, self-care, couple time you inevitably experience when a baby is born?

54. What kinds of things could both of you do to help one another cope with this part of the transition to parenthood?

55. How can the two of you continue to connect if you cannot have the same life that you had before baby? What kinds of new date ideas can you think of? Get creative!

56. Who do you think you would trust the most to adequately care for your baby so you can get a date night? You both have to agree on this person. Bonus points if you can think of more than one person.

57. How do you want to bring up your feelings of needing more time together? How do you want to bring up your needs for independent time?

58. Which one of you is going to take on the role of planning post-baby dates?

59. What are your thoughts on kid-free vacations?

The What Are We Going to Do with Them War

60. From what you remember, how did your own parents discipline you when you were a child? What was your perception of that discipline? What parts of your parent's discipline strategies would you like to model and what would you like to change when thinking about disciplining your own children?

61. What is something your parents used to say or do to you during a discipline interaction that you hated?

62. What is something your parents used to say or do to you during a discipline interaction that you respected or even liked?

63. What are your thoughts on the idea that parents should be able to control their children's behavior? What does it mean to have effective discipline? What does "effective" mean to you?

64. How early do you think that discipline should start with children?

65. What kinds of discipline strategies do you think are effective?

66. What kinds of discipline strategies do you think are not effective?

67. What kinds of discipline strategies do you think should be avoided at all costs?

68. What do you believe is an appropriate age for each discipline strategy you agreed upon? How will you deal with toddlers, elementary school aged children, middle school kiddos, and high schoolers? Are there certain discipline techniques that you believe are age-specific? Are there certain discipline strategies that you believe can be used with children of all ages?

69. What sorts of behaviors do you think require discipline no matter the circumstance? For example: talking back, interrupting, breaking something, going against an established family rule, foul language, etc.

70. Do you see yourself more as a good cop or a bad cop? Which of these roles would you rather take on? Or would you like to work really hard at not taking on these roles at all?

71. What kind of disciplinarian do you want to be? What kind of disciplinarian to you want your partner to be? What is your ideal situation?

72. How do you think you'll cope with your discipline plan "working" with one child and not with another child?

73. What are your opinions about yelling at children?

74. What kinds of things could both of you do to help one another cope with this conflict-inducing part of parenthood?

75. How do you want to bring up your feelings of dissatisfaction with discipline?

"Be more empathic. Sometimes, misunderstanding and/or conflict with your partner can be explained by taking a look at (and then being sensitive to) your partner's past experiences, core personality traits, and upbringing."

Dr. Jennie Rosier
@RelationshipsLoveHappiness

Chapter Eight:
Gaining Even More Perspective

Have you ever struggled to understand your partner? Maybe you were in an argument and your partner was overly-sensitive (in your opinion) to something that you said or maybe your mate laughed out loud at something that you took very seriously or maybe you thought something was a big deal and your partner trivialized it. Whatever the circumstance, we have all felt this way at some point or another. Why did he respond like that? How was I supposed to know what she *really* meant? How did he get *that* from our conversation? How did she not understand my point of view? Believe me, I know the feeling. It seems like my husband and I are habitually working towards understanding each other's points of view. And no, you **cannot** just chalk it up to the idea that Men are From Mars and Women are from Venus! It just doesn't work that way. Men and women are WAY more similar than the media and our culture would lead you to believe. Anyways, that's another topic for another book.

From one partner simply getting the wrong idea about what the other partner wanted for a birthday present to a ridiculously huge, drawn-out argument about how one partner was seriously offended by the other, numerous problems can be caused by these communication faux-pas.

Sometimes, these misunderstandings can be explained by taking a look at (and then being sensitive to) your partner's past experiences, core personality traits, and upbringing. In fact, an individual's upbringing significantly contributes to how that person develops their communication style, ability to hone communication skills, and general approach to communication interactions. For instance, if your partner was raised in a house where conflict was typically avoided (or not allowed), it is likely very difficult for your partner to first, have an argument, and second, learn to effectively engage in constructive conflict. Similarly, if your mate was brought up to openly express their mushy emotions, this may be one of the reasons why your partner wants to say "I love you" 683 times a day or wants to use cutesy nicknames or wants to have discussions about your feelings and the state of your relationship on a regular basis. Thus, looking back over your partner's upbringing can shed some light on why your partner behaves in certain ways.

Below are some research-based connections found between parental behaviors and a child's internalization of those behaviors; which tend to impact them well into adulthood. Hopefully, they can help you gain some insight into the root causes of your own communication efforts and help you better understand why your partner communicates in certain ways.

First, when there is a significant amount of arguing (between parent and child or between both parents) in the home, children tend to grow up into adults who can:[54]

- develop issues with abandonment and fears for personal safety because they are frightened by what they are experiencing.
- develop low self-esteem because they blame themselves for the arguments.
- develop anger problems, with males typically lashing out on others and females typically lashing out on themselves.
- not be able to trust others because they were not able to become close with one or both of their parents.
- experience low-grade, long-term depression.
- have a difficult time understanding physical and verbal boundaries because they saw their violent parent violate other people's boundaries and it became the norm for them.

Second, when a parent engages in criticism of other people (whether the criticized persons are strangers, friends, family members, the other parent, or the child), children tend to grow into adults who can:[55]

- develop feelings of self-hate because they feel as though they are not good enough and are not able to do anything correctly.
- learn to not trust themselves and question decisions that they have made.
- develop low self-esteem because again, they blame themselves for the criticism (even when the critical remarks are not directed toward themselves).
- undermine and underestimate themselves in personal relationships.
- become either overly dependent on or overly independent from a romantic partner.

Third, when families move around a lot (either from house to house, from city to city, from state to state, or from country to country) or just once because of some traumatic event (such as a house fire, natural disaster, death of a parent, divorce, or the like) children could grow into adults who could:[56]

- develop fears of abandonment because they're repeatedly leaving their group of friends, family members, and surroundings. Later in life, these people tend to not welcome change (because things changed so much for them as children) and may not make new friends easily (because they feel like those people would probably leave them anyway, so working on a new friendship not worth the trouble).
- suffer in school. In fact, studies show that, children who move frequently are more likely to have problems at school.
- become depressed or develop other anxiety disorders.

Lastly, when one or both parents fail to emotionally respond, respond in a negative manner, or respond inconsistently to a child during times of distress (including simple things like falling down and scraping a knee, going to the doctor, being frustrated with a task, waking up in the middle of the night, being sick, or more serious stressful events like having close family members become sick, having a parent become incarcerated, experiencing parental divorce, experiencing the death of someone close to them, etc.), children can grow into adults who develop lowered stress thresholds and insecure attachment.

Stressful childhood events require caring, loving attention from important adults in a child's life. The impact that your own childhood stress has on you now as an adult is largely based on two factors: the presence of supportive, caring adults in your life and the severity and frequency of the stress that you were experiencing. Researchers at Harvard's Center for the Developing Child[57] have extensively studied how different types of stress impact brain development. They've identified three main categories of stress: positive, tolerable, and toxic. As explained by their 2014 report, "Learning how to cope with mild or moderate stress is an important part of healthy child development. When faced with novel or threatening situations, our bodies respond by increasing our heart rate, blood pressure, and stress hormones, such as cortisol. When a young child's stress response systems are activated in the context of supportive relationships with adults, these physiological effects are buffered and return to baseline levels. The result is the development of healthy stress response systems. However, if the stress response is extreme, long-lasting, and buffering relationships are unavailable to the child, the result can be toxic stress, leading to damaged, weakened bodily systems and brain architecture, with lifelong repercussions" (p. 1).

> Extreme exposure to toxic stress can change the stress system so that it responds at lower thresholds to events that might not be stressful to others, and, therefore, the stress response system activates more frequently and for longer periods than is necessary. This wear and tear increases the risk of stress-related physical and mental illness later in life.
>
> (Harvard Study, 2014)

If you or your spouse experienced toxic stress as a child, parenthood is unfortunately going to be much more difficult for you. "Extreme exposure to toxic stress can change the stress system so that it responds at lower thresholds to events that might not be stressful to others, and, therefore, the stress response system activates more frequently and for longer periods than is necessary, like revving a car engine for hours every day."[58] Imagine listening to your new baby crying for what seems like forever and not being able to take it. The sound gets under your skin and it makes you really stressed out. And then there's your partner. Totally fine. The crying doesn't get to them. So now, you're not only stressed out by the crying, but you're also stressed by the fact that your partner is unphased. What the hell?!

You likely have a lower stress threshold than your mate. This threshold could have been lowered after you experienced toxic stress as an infant, toddler, school-aged child, or teen. You might know exactly what the toxic stress entailed and you might not. For example, the crying could unconsciously trigger something inside yourself that reminds your brain of the incessant crying you did as an infant. You might not remember, but your brain does.

Childhood stress and how parents respond to children during these experiences can also impact one's adult attachment. As I mentioned earlier in this book, attachment theory contends that "the nature of early interactions with a caregiver will inform young children's neurological internal working models, which influence the nature of their interpersonal relationships well into adulthood."[59]

Your attachment style can easily impact your ability to maintain your relationship while trying to cope with the demands of parenthood. For example, if you experience significant attachment anxiety as an adult, it might be more difficult for you to bring up concerns you have to your partner because you fear that if you cause a problem, they could leave you. Or, if you experience a good amount of attachment avoidance, you might not want to bring up an issue you're having because you don't feel comfortable sharing your feelings about serious things. Ignoring the relational distress you're experiencing can cause additional problems in your relationship that could be quite difficult to repair.

In adulthood, attachment is measured by the amount of anxiety and the amount of avoidance one experiences in romantic relationships. This anxiety and avoidance combine in different ways to create a person's adult attachment style, which researchers typically identify as four styles: secure (low anxiety, low avoidance), anxious preoccupied (high anxiety, low avoidance), dismissive avoidant (low anxiety, high avoidance), and fearful avoidant (high anxiety, high avoidance). Most people do not actually fit nicely into one of these groups. Instead, many have a primary attachment style with some behavioral tendencies from one (or more) of the other styles. For instance, you might be securely attached with some dismissive tendencies. This would mean that in most situations and with most relationship partners, you feel secure. But sometimes, or with certain relationship partners, you might feel less secure. If you have dismissive tendencies, you might feel like you need more space or independence from your partner or you might go as far as feeling like you don't even need your partner.

What's your attachment? Do a little self-reflection and answer the following couple of questions before reading the descriptions on the next set of pages. Then, see if you fit into one of these descriptions.

1) How positively do you view yourself? Do you view yourself as more amazing, terrible, or somewhere in the middle? 2) How positively do you view other people? Do you think most people are more good-intentioned, out to screw you over, or somewhere in the middle?

4 ADULT ATTACHMENT CATEGORIES

SECURE: LOW ANXIETY & LOW AVOIDANCE

Experiencing low anxiety and low avoidance, securely attached adults are typically comfortable with both intimacy and independence. They enjoy sharing personal information about themselves and listening to their partner self-discloseto build intimacy, but they also value their autonomy and respect the autonomy of their partners. Adults with secure attachment styles do not often worry about their partners cheating on, judging, accepting, or abandoning on them; they are confident in their self-worth and feel secure in their relationships. They tend to have positive opinions of themselves and of others. While not always the case, many secure adults are also highly sociable; being able to "hold a conversation with anyone."

DISMISSIVE: LOW ANXIETY & HIGH AVOIDANCE

Experiencing low anxiety and high avoidance, dismissive adults typically try to avoid getting too close to others in romantic relationships. Additionally, they can crave independence and might even claim that they don't need a romantic partner to be happy and/or feel fulfilled. Dismissive adults tend to have a high opinion of themselves and a low opinion of others; hence their typical feelings that they don't need a partner- not many people live up to the standards they have set for themselves. When dismissive adults actually find themselves in a relationship, they tend to not openly express their feelings or emotions, want to take things slow, and are typically "not ready to commit" as soon as their partners. One might hear a dismissive person cynically say something like, "True love isn't real," which could be one reason why they are reluctant to start relationships. In order to distance themselves (consciously or unconsciously) from a mate, they might focus on small imperfections, pull away when things are going well, check out mentally, avoid physical closeness, and/or keep secrets.

FEARFUL: HIGH ANXIETY & HIGH AVOIDANCE

Experiencing high anxiety and high avoidance, fearful (sometimes labeled "fearful- avoidant") adults typically want intimacy in romantic relationships, but tend to have a difficult time trusting others. This dissonance can cause significant stress in an individual. Their desire for intimacy and their fear of sharing emotions work against each other; making it difficult for fearful-avoidants to form healthy relationships with others. They tend to have negative opinions of themselves and negative opinions of others. Fearful individuals are typically hypersensitive to social approval and might avoid social situations because of the fear that others are negatively judging them. When in relationships, fearful individuals might emotionally retreat (especially during difficult conversations), self-deprecate (as they view themselves as unworthy), express jealousy (due to their trust issues), experience separation anxiety, become consumed with a serious relationship partner, and worry about getting hurt if they get too close.

ANXIOUS: HIGH ANXIETY & LOW AVOIDANCE

Experiencing high anxiety and low avoidance, anxious-preoccupied adults typically want intimacy in romantic relationships, but tend to become dependent on others. Additionally, they can become obsessive when in a relationship, have a strong desire for approval from their mates, and tend to be worried about their partners abandoning them, judging them, and/or accepting them. Anxious-preoccupied adults can have a low opinion of themselves and a high opinion of others. They tend to be very comfortable sharing their emotions and might even overshare in order to increase relational intimacy faster than the norm. When in relationships, anxious adults might easily become jealous, make seemingly constant requests for a partner's help with tasks or for emotional comfort and excessively make requests for hugging and/or kissing. They often focus a lot of their energy on gaining approval from others; sometimes at the expense of their own desires and values.

Taken together, these are just a few outcomes of early childhood experiences. Sadly, many of these outcomes continue to impact people throughout adolescence and adulthood. This is not to say that people are **unable** to change. People can and do change. It happens every day, in fact. But, more often than not, some, if not all, of the outcomes that have been ingrained in the brains of individuals from their childhoods remain relatively stable over the lifespan.

What can you do to combat the arguments that may arise from differing childhood experiences? Gain some perspective. Try to put yourself in your partner's shoes. And let's be clear, I'm not advising you to just think about how you would react. Putting yourself in your partner's shoes is more complex than that. When you do this well, you stand where your partner is standing, in their shoes, with all of their life experiences, trauma, personality, and baggage in your mind. This is not about how YOU would feel (with all of your past experiences, personality, relationships, baggage, etc.) in the moment; it's about YOUR PARTNER. It's about someone other than you. That's perspective-taking.

Let's say that you feel like your partner was overly sensitive to your recent teasing about how your partner cares for your newborn. You recognize that your partner is upset and then reflect on their past experiences. When you begin to realize that your partner's overly critical parent may have made them more sensitive to your teasing (even if your remarks were well-intentioned), you're engaging in perceptual empathy (i.e. perceiving the situation that your partner is facing). Then, when you really begin to think about how it must have been very difficult to be criticized by a parent (one of the only people in the world who should have unconditional love and affection for you) you're engaging in cognitive empathy (i.e. putting yourself in their shoes). Finally, when you consider how your mate must have felt as a child when they were criticized by a parent *and* how they felt when another person whom they trust made a comment that could be

> "I urge you to please notice when you are happy, and exclaim or murmur or think at some point, 'If this isn't nice, I don't know what is.'"
>
> –Kurt Vonnegut

interpreted as criticism (even if it wasn't intended that way), you're engaging in affective empathy.

Understanding that you and your partner likely communicate and behave in certain ways based on your own childhood experiences can teach you a lot about each other. Maybe you used to look at your partner's jealousy expression negatively and now you realize that it likely has little to do with you and everything to do with some childhood trauma they experienced and cannot get past. Or maybe you used to see your partner's emotional brick wall as a huge roadblock and potential red flag/deal breaker in your relationship and now you realize that your mate has such a hard time talking about difficult topics because their parents struggled to tend to their needs in a consistent manner in childhood. Whatever the revelation is, I hope that this information has made you more empathic towards the close people in your life and better able to provide them with effective emotional support when they really need it.

Speaking of emotional support, that's another one of my absolute favorite topics.

So many times, someone you love (a partner, parent, friend, or child) reacts to something in a way that you think is over-the-top. Maybe you think your mate is exaggerating his anger when someone cuts him off while driving, or you think your child is being overly dramatic after fighting with his sibling over a toy, or you think your friend is way too sad after breaking free from a terrible relationship. Whatever the situation, it is extremely common to find yourself feeling the urge to say, "get over it" or "calm down" when someone you love is feeling hurt in some way.

Hard truth: your opinion of their reaction is irrelevant. It. Does. Not. Matter. Sorry for being so blunt, but it is. Everyone experiences life differently (hopefully you've figured that out by now) and the fact of the matter is that your loved one is feeling something. That's what matters— someone YOU LOVE is feeling something. Regardless of how you think you would have reacted, SOMEONE YOU LOVE is sad/angry/depressed/offended/scared.

Your loved one's feelings are REAL. And they are feeling these feelings for a reason.

No matter why your loved one is upset, there are some research-based ways to effectively support them.[60] But before you actually start trying to support someone, you really need to change your perspective about your goal in this interaction. I used to think that I needed to help my distressed love ones by solving their problems and that solving their problems would make them feel better. I now know that problem-solving and improved feelings should NOT be the main goals of emotional support. Most people just want someone to be there for them during a rough time. And further, depending on the distressful event, most people are not going to suddenly feel better after talking with you.

The REAL GOAL of emotional support is to make someone feel connected to you. Like they have someone they can count on and trust. Someone who won't judge them, who will validate their feelings, and will give them their time. Sure, some people will directly ask you, "what should I do?!" In that case, some advice might be warranted (but, tread lightly). But for the most part, people just want connection.

Here's a graphic outlining all of those research-based steps from Dr. Brant Burleson, my Ph.D. advisor, emotional support expert, and one of the most prolific interpersonal communication scholars in the discipline:

how to provide effective
emotional support

CHANGE YOUR GOAL:
It's not your job to make someone feel better.
Instead, it's your job to make someone feel connected to you.

1 Motivate the distressed person to tell and re-tell his or her story

4 Encourage the expression of thoughts and feelings that they experienced during and after the situation

2 Ask questions about the problem so that the distressed person can elaborate

5 Acknowledge and legitimize the distressed person's thoughts and feelings

3 Be actively engaged in the conversation

6 Let them know that you understand why they feel that way

things to avoid

DO NOT discuss your own experiences
DO NOT evaluate their feelings or the other people involved in the situation
DO NOT ignore the person's feelings by trying to help them look at the bright side
DO NOT tell the person what they should do or how they should feel
DO NOT distract the person's attention from their feelings

Providing better emotional support can get you on the path to true empathy. True empathy involves more than being sympathetic to your loved one's feelings. It involves more than feeling sorry for or pitying them. It involves more than feeling bad about what happened to them as a child. And, it involves more than simply wanting them to be happy. True empathy is about feeling WITH another person, it's about understanding their less-than-desirable behaviors or reaction to the world, and it's about accepting them for who they are, what their feeling, and how they're coping with it all. Empathy is tough, but essential to a healthy relationship.

I get that memorizing the 6 tips described in the Burleson-inspired graphic can be difficult to do. So, here are three easy-to-remember phrases that I believe are essential when dealing with other people's emotions (whether you think they're warranted or not). And yes, these phrases work with everyone—your partner, friends, family and children!

"I'm always here for you."

This sentence can do wonders for any relationship. Remember that the goal of emotional support is to help someone feel connected to you. Knowing that someone is there for you, whenever you need them, is so empowering. These kinds of affirmations are nice to hear during stressful times. Personally, I have worked diligently (albeit not perfectly) at replacing all of my "calm down" phrases with "I'm always here for you." When you know that you don't have to go-it-alone, you begin to feel more secure in your relationship and with your feelings.

"You have every right to feel this way."

I can't tell you how many times I say this phrase to people. And when I do, a visible sense of calm rushes over them. A sense that they aren't crazy; that they aren't being realistic. The sense of calm that comes with feeling completely validated. Again, it's an empowering feeling.

"I'm glad you're talking to me about this."

If you don't know what to say, say this. People want to feel connected to others. They want to feel valued, loved, and safe. When you tell someone that you're happy they're talking to you about something that could be difficult for them to talk to you about, you're letting them know that your relationship is a safe place for them to share, be open, and be free of judgement. Again, it's empowering.

Anytime your partner is stressed out, overwhelmed, or burned out, make sure you listen to their story, avoid giving advice, encourage them to elaborate, validate their feelings, and whatever you do, avoid telling them to "calm down." Try to empathize with them. Be gentle. Know that most of our behaviors have little to do with other people and more often than not, they have everything to do with what's going on in our own bodies, our ability to cope with stress, and our ability to recognize how our actions impact others. Empathy is an important skill to have in life, and it's especially important when you're navigating your way through a romantic relationship while adjusting to parenthood.

"While Gottman's Four Horsemen can definitely be signs of impending doom, the individuals who give up on fixing their relationship are the ones experiencing the real apocalypse."

Dr. Jennie Rosier
@RelationshipsLoveHappiness

Chapter Nine:
Fighting a Fair Fight

"Conflict is an unavoidable fact of life."[61] Everyone does it, few like talking about it, and hardly anyone enjoys it. And as you've been reading up to this point, the warfare that can develop after a baby arrives has the potential to cause two people who supposedly love one another to say things they don't mean, do things they regret, and even ruin their relationship. For decades, researchers have recognized that these conversations are extremely sensitive and difficult, and they've subsequently discovered a variety of ways to best go about initiating, engaging in, and ending arguments; which can make your life a whole lot easier.

> Marital conflict can be about virtually anything.
>
> (Fincham, 2003)

Before we get into what effective conflict actually entails, I think it's important to revisit the argument I've been trying to create throughout this lovely little book: You can never fully prepare for everything that's going to happen to yourself, your partner, your relationship, or the life you share together after a baby is born, but adjusting your expectations and creating a plan for dealing with all of the inevitable stress you're going to experience is one way to begin this journey on the right foot.

As I've said before and I'll say again later, be gentle with yourself. You can spend years preparing for something and still mess it all up from time to time. And that is okay. Life isn't perfect... and neither are you. You can't prepare for everything. In fact, no one can. Learning about the common arguments many couples face and creating a new set of realistic expectations can help, but there's no guarantee that you won't experience drama.

Since these conflicts are inevitable and the perils of relationship war can be dire, learning how to fight a fair fight is key to saving your relationship from any casualties. To help you figure it all out, this chapter is going to cover how to prepare for conflict, what to say, do, and avoid when you're in the thick of it, and how to effectively apologize when you say or do something you regret.

Preparing for Conflict

Preparing for conflict is a great first step. You've already got more realistic expectations for post-baby drama about chores, sex, gatekeeping, time, and discipline. And you've hopefully talked about these issues with your partner; another vital component of preparing. Lucky for you, chapter seven included 75 conversation-starters to get those discussions started. If you haven't had those conversations yet, know that they can be really beneficial when you're trying to understand your partner's parenting values and beliefs.

What else can you do to help you and your partner better navigate starting a family? Well, I've got two more expectations for you to put on your list. First, it's important to recognize that some conflict will happen regardless of how much you talk about it, promise to avoid it, or think it's not a big deal. Everyone deals with stress differently and even the same person could deal with the same stress differently at different times in their life. Life is complicated. Some situations trigger us when we didn't ever think they would and sometimes we react in ways we never expected. Try your best to be loving even in the face of anger and frustration, be gentle with yourself when you behave in ways that you're not proud of, and promise to reconcile when you mess up.

A second really important expectation to recognize is that some of your conflict will never be solved. You read that right—some of your conflict will continue to come up as problems in your relationship for years to come. As Dr. John Gottman would say, most problematic issues in marriages (about 69%, in fact) don't ever get *solved*. Instead, the majority of problems are *managed* by romantic partners. This is vital to truly understanding conflict in romantic relationships. Simply having conflict does not mean that your relationship is doomed. Conflict is an essential component of happy, healthy partnerships. It's about how you handle it. But, if you experience and engage in a significant amount of destructive conflict that demeans, demoralizes, offends, or ignores one or both partners, you need to turn things around before your relationship begins to deteriorate.

> Approximately 69% of relationship conflict are perpetual problems.
>
> (Gottman, 1999)

Make a vow to recognize when you're getting upset, bring it up with each other in a loving, constructive way, and promise to either work hard at working it out or decide to manage it by agreeing to disagree.

The Actual Fight

Well, today is the day. It's happening. Your first post-baby argument. Maybe your partner didn't take out the trash for the seventh time and it's piling up on the counter which is making you feel like you have to do everything, or maybe you really need some self-care time so you don't lose your mind and you've brought it up in a not-so-kind way, or maybe your partner complained about how you don't want to BLEEP him anymore and it's making him feel undesirable, disconnected, and unloved. Whatever the cause of the conflict, it's here.

When conflict arises in a relationship, individuals have several decisions to make about how they are going to communicate with one another. Researchers tend to talk about conflict in terms of how constructive or how destructive these choices are; with most conflict interactions ebbing and flowing from one side of this continuum to the other during the course of a single interaction. Constructive conflict involves cooperation, support, flexibility, compromise or negotiation, and de-escalation.[62] Conversely, destructive conflict is characterized by competition, inflexibility, escalation, domination, defensiveness, and cross complaining.

One of these roads is clearly an easier road to take than the other. Destructiveness doesn't take a whole lot of effort on your part. It's easy to become defensive, to try and dominate a conversation, to yell at your partner about their upset, or to be stubborn and stand your ground no matter what is said. But (albeit much more difficult, time-consuming, effort-requiring) constructive conflict is far better for you and your relationship. In order to maintain a constructive tone, you and your partner need to work hard at learning to complain, owning up to your own faults, de-escalating, picking your battles, and paying attention to your words; while simultaneously avoiding criticism, yelling, getting defensive, blaming, threatening, mocking, and the like.

Lay Off the Criticism and Learn to Complain

"Criticism from a trusted and loved person can bread feelings of self-hate in the target of the criticism."

–Jennie Rosier, Ph.D.

Unfortunately, many relationships are consumed by criticism. Whether you're consistently knocking how your partner does the laundry, slamming your partner's daily choice of clothing, or always pointing out your partner's inability to be on time, criticism is a nasty communication technique that, when built up over time, can seriously damage your relationship.

It's important to note that there's a difference between complaining about your partner's actions one day and criticizing your partner's character. Where complaints can sometimes be helpful (allowing people to take note and possibly make a change), criticism tends to attack a person's disposition by blaming and generalizing the issue beyond the behavior in question. For instance, "I felt like you didn't support me yesterday when I was sad" is an example of a complaint; while "You never support me" would be an example of criticism. Using words like "always" and "never" represent a critical remark. Try to remove those terms from your vocabulary when talking about the actions of your partner.

Researchers agree with the idea that criticism tends to have negative outcomes. In fact, criticism has been linked to feelings of embarrassment[63] and lower relationship satisfaction[64] within the person being criticized. Furthermore, when comparing communication patterns of happy and unhappy couples, researchers have discovered that distressed couples tend to exhibit more negative verbal behaviors like sarcasm and criticism than happier couples.[65] Dr. John Gottman has even named criticism as one of his "Four Horseman of the Apocalypse" when talking about the four signs which can reveal that couples are headed for break-up or divorce (defensiveness, contempt, and stonewalling being the other three).[66]

How can you change your critical ways? According to Dr. John Gottman and Nan Silver,[67] learning to **complain** more effectively may be able to take the place of criticism. Effective complaining involves identifying *one* specific behavior by your partner that you are unhappy with and not allowing yourself to generalize the issue beyond the behavior in question. Something like, "I felt like I didn't get the help I needed today when you got home from work. I had been with the baby all day and I really needed to not do the dishes." However, you still don't want to complain all of the time. Quit your pickin', learn to complain more effectively, and you can be on the road to more constructive conflict.

Avoid Defensiveness and Stonewalling

Defensiveness is usually a response people have during conflict where they shift the blame to someone or something else, whine about what is being said to them, offer more complaints and criticism to their partners, or make excuses for their behaviors. Instead of becoming defensive, individuals in healthy relationships will accept a complaint from a partner and try to work towards a solution. Remember, your partner is coming to you for a reason. And sometimes, it's difficult for us to figure out why our mate would be upset about something. In these situations, it's important for you to listen and try to understand your partner's point of view.

To avoid defensiveness, Dr. John Gottman offers a few steps. First, when your mate is initiating conflict with you, try to be calm. Getting excited or angered won't help the situation. Second, listen to what your mate is saying. If you listen carefully, you'll probably be able to understand what your partner is actually upset about. Lastly, try to respond non-defensively. Gottman and Silver argue, "we need to ignore what's being said about us and learn to hear our partner's negativity as an attempt to underline how strongly she or he feels about the problem and what desperate measures are being employed to get us to pay attention."[68]

> "Even in stable, happy relationships, when conflict begins with hostility, defensive sequences result."
>
> –John Gottman, Ph.D.
> *The Science of Trust*

Instead of getting defensive, try acknowledging and validating your partner's concerns. Imagine that your partner comes to you with a complaint. Something that has apparently upset that rather badly. Many times, your first reaction in this situation is to explain your true intentions were never to hurt your loved one, "I didn't mean to hurt your feelings. You shouldn't be this upset because I never intended to upset you." Interestingly, your opinion of the situation is actually irrelevant. Sure, you can tell your loved one that you never intended to hurt them, BUT that should be reserved for later in the conversation... or never. Your job here is not to defend yourself. Your partner's feelings are real. Your partner is feeling them. For a reason. In this situation, your job is to acknowledge that you hurt/upset/angered your partner ("I can see that this really upset you."), validate their feelings ("I get it. You have every right to feel upset. I would probably be upset if you did this to me."), and apologize ("I'm sorry that I made you feel this way.").

Sometimes, avoiding conflict can turn into stonewalling; which is also one of Gottman's *Four Horsemen of the Apocalypse*. Emotional distance, ignoring one another, being unresponsive in conversations, and giving someone the silent treatment are all examples of stonewalling. Stonewalling is a good sign of a troubled relationship. To avoid stonewalling your partner, engage in behaviors like eye contact, head nods, and physical gestures to show you're interested. If your partner is stonewalling you, you may want to begin talking about where your relationship is heading with him or her.

> Members of happy, stable relationships do exhibit criticism, defensiveness, and stonewalling occasionally; however, repair is what keeps the relationships healthy by promoting interest in each other, affection for each other, and humor, while lowering stress and perceived tension.
>
> (Goldberg, 2017)

Overall, you need to work hard at addressing conflict without becoming defensive or stonewalling one another. Owning up to your faults (even if you don't always agree) can actually start making things better.

Quit Yelling and De-Escalate

While most arguments don't usually *begin* as a screaming match, many end up that way. In fact, many disagreements (but certainly not all) start off about seemingly insignificant topics or at the least begin with partners behaving in a civil manner— speaking calmly, at an average rate and volume, and using acceptable language. Sadly, arguments can quickly escalate and turn into larger-than-life wars between romantic partners where yelling, name-calling, insulting, and criticism are common. The fact of the matter is that *any* argument where escalation takes place (and de-escalation does not) is considered destructive.

If you're in an argument with your partner and you can see that things are getting out of hand, there's still hope. You can easily turn conflict around by learning how to de-escalate the conversation. Below are a three sample statements that you can say to attempt to de-escalate your feud.

> "Okay, let's take a 10-minute (or 10 hour) break, cool down, and then work towards actually solving this problem."

Stepping away from a disagreement, taking a break, and coming back to the issue at a later date (FYI: you have to actually come back to it) allows people to calm down and think about what they really want to talk about. Many times, people are able to better organize their thoughts and express their feelings more effectively after taking a break. But beware; continuously tabling a discussion is not a good idea. You have to eventually work it out. And, sooner is better than later.

> "Wait a minute. What are we really fighting about?"

At times, it's vital that you ask yourself (and your partner) this exact question. Couples have tendencies to engage in what I like to call *cryptic arguing* where they seem to be arguing about one topic when in fact, they are really upset about something totally unrelated. For instance, you might be angry at your partner about comments made by him or her a week earlier. Instead of talking about how those comments made you feel, you become easily agitated when your mate leaves his or her dirty clothes on the floor. You erupt in anger about the clothes when it's really about the comment made a week prior. Or, you might not be mad at your mate at all. Maybe you're stressed out at work or with the kids and you take it out on your partner for something rather trivial. I think that this happens a lot with couples who have children. For instance, when our twins were infants, my husband and I would argue about the most ridiculous things. "Don't put your soda on the fucking table! You're going to leave a stain! You always do shit like that!" And that wasn't all. "Why can't you figure this out? It's like you're not even trying" was another phrase of ours. At a certain point during these conflicts, one of us would sometimes ask, "What the hell are we really fighting about? Why are we so upset about this?" Saying something like this in a light-hearted tone can easily break the tension during an impassioned quarrel.

> "I love you and you love me.
> Why are we talking to each other like this?"

This one is my favorite and my go-to during times of destruction. Insults, name-calling, negative sarcasm, and other forms of contempt are commonplace in many disagreements between romantic partners. Reiterating your love for one another can put your conversation in perspective. I know when my husband and I have used this strategy, one of the next sentences is something like, "You're right. I don't want to fight with you. I'm sorry." And then we're able to think more rationally and work through the issue.

If you really love someone, that kind of hurtful language should not be part of your relationship vocabulary to begin with. But if it sneaks in somehow, you can quickly nip those detrimental conversations in the bud (and de-escalate your conflict) by shifting the focus of your discussion. Emphasizing your love can cause you and your partner to quit using destructive tactics, remember that you actually care for one another, and maybe even help you solve (or agree to maintain) your problems.

Pick Your Battles

One of the better pieces of advice given to me over the years is that whenever you're in a relationship, it's important to pick your battles. Relationships aren't any fun when you're arguing or picking on each other all of the time.

Take the time to really think about the importance of something before you make the decision to bring it up. Try your hardest to not sweat the small stuff. This difficult phase of parenthood will pass and you want to make your relationship survives it.

Learning to complain instead of criticize can help with this, but complaining all of the time doesn't really help either. Think about the many insignificant battles that you and your mate have and try to cut a few of them out.

I'm always amazed by the amount of people who *seem* to understand how mean and terrible their language can be, yet continue to use destructive communication strategies in heated (and even not-so-heated) interactions with their partners. For example, I know a couple where both parties consistently tell one another to "fuck off" when in an argument. Now I'm surely not the swear-word police (I'm a bit rough around the edges myself), but I have NEVER EVER said "fuck you" to my husband or told him to go fuck himself or anything remotely like that. I would never stoop to that level of disrespect with him. And he has never said anything that disrespectful to me. That kind of language is just not part of our relationship's vocabulary. Cursing **around** your partner is completely different from cursing **at** your partner.

"Gratitude is the healthiest of all human emotions. The more you express gratitude for what you have, the more likely you will have even more to express gratitude for."

–Zig Ziglar
Author, *Born to Win*

Name-calling, using negative humor, threatening your partner or the status of your relationship, giving ultimatums, belittling your partner's ideas and thoughts, and bossing your partner around are a few more poor choices. If you want your relationship to succeed, these negative communication patterns need to be completely eliminated from your interactions.

Add more positive language into your normal, everyday talks and your conflict interactions. You could work hard towards frequently expressing your love, interest, gratitude, and commitment for your partner, to your partner.

The next page has a great breakdown of constructive conflict tips; including some ideas about what to say, what to do, and what to avoid.

CONSTRUCTIVE CONFLICT TIPS

WHAT TO SAY

-Validate your partner's feelings, "You have every right to feel this way."
-Acknowledge your partner's upset, "You're really frustrated."
-De-escalate the conflict, "I love you and you love me. Why are we talking to each other like this?"
-Remind your partner of your commitment, "I want to work through this with you. I'm here for all of this."

WHAT TO DO

-Maintain your calm by keeping a supportive, loving tone in your voice
-Remember that you love your partner
-Be flexible when the conversation takes an unexpected turn
-Listen to your partner
-Try to address one problem at a time

WHAT TO AVOID

-Eliminate "always" and "never" from your vocabulary when talking about your partner's behavior
-Avoid getting defensive when your partner comes to you with a complaint
-Avoid yelling or even raising your voice
-Avoid contempt, mocking, or eye-rolling
-Avoid giving threats, ultimatums, or sarcasm
-Avoid making excuses, whining, shifting blame, or countering with your own criticism

Crafting Your Apology

So, you got into an argument and you're feeling the need to apologize. Maybe you did something you said you wouldn't do, or you didn't do something you said you would do, or you just flat out hurt your spouse's feelings and now you want to make amends. Well many times, a simple "I'm sorry" just ain't gonna cut it. And then you're still in trouble. Below are four easy (well, mostly easy) steps to go alongside all of the other constructive conflict advice I've outlined in this chapter.

1 **Listen to your partner's concerns and feelings.** Listening is one of the most powerful tools in your relationship toolkit. Really. Let your mate talk about anything related to the behavior in question and pay attention to everything your mate is saying. Try to understand where your partner is coming from. Put yourself in his or her shoes and begin to recognize how your actions impacted your partner. Let your partner elaborate as much as he or she wants and acknowledge his or her feelings. You can ask questions if you need clarification. But be careful, make sure that you phrase your questions so that they imply that you actually want to understand your partner, not as if you are trying to discredit your partner's emotions or point of view.

2 **Admit your faults.** Take responsibility for your actions, even if you think that your partner is wrong, exaggerating, or out-of-line in their accusations. The fact of the matter is that even if your intentions were not to purposely hurt your mate, you did. There was some miscommunication between what you meant to do or say and how your mate perceived what you did or said. In fact, miscommunication is one of the leading causes of conflict in relationships. So, if you hurt your partner, recognize that. You can still say that it wasn't your intention to upset them, but it's important to take ownership for how your partner is feeling.

3 **Offer up a plan.** Apologies are rather useless if you don't plan to change your behavior. And many times, the plan is clear— "Okay, I promise to do the dishes so you don't have that chore on your plate." But other times, the plan is not as clear.

This is where the two of you need to work together to come up with a solution to your problem. You could ask your partner, "How can I fix this?" or "I really don't want you to be sad/angry with me anymore. What can I do?" Again, you need to listen to what your mate says and then decide what you're willing and able to do. And if the plan is to "not do _____" ever again or less often, think of a positive, more desirable behavior to put in its place. Ending bad habits is so much easier when you replace it with a good habit. However you decide to do it, making a clear plan for the future is an excellent way to get through this tough time with your partner.

4 **Don't do it again.** This seems like a no-brainer, but I can't tell you how many times my husband or I will say that we're sorry about something and then go ahead and do the upsetting act again; sometimes only days later. It's terrible, actually. If you plan to not do something and then you do it again, what kind of message does that send to your partner? I'll tell you. It says that you were less-than-sincere in your original apology. It says that you don't have enough respect for the future plan your both made together. And it says that you don't value your relationship enough to stop doing whatever it is that hurt your partner in the first place. To put it another way, if you do it again, it makes it very difficult for your partner to forgive you and it could cause resentment.

Overall, conflict *should* play a role in your relationship. It's inevitable. You will argue. You will fight. You might even say things you don't mean. But in the end, you need to be willing to acknowledge and respect your mate's point of view and try to work toward a solution in a loving, supportive, flexible way. And don't sweat the small stuff.

"I promise to try to go with the flow when things don't go as planned."

Dr. Jennie Rosier

@RelationshipsLoveHappiness

Chapter Ten:
Creating a Shared Parenting Vision

Now that you've talked and talked and talked about anything and everything related to the five most common post-baby conflicts and thought about how your own and your partner's past experiences have shaped who you are today, it's time to create a shared parenting vision; which can help you realize the family and relationship of your dreams. Having a shared idea about your future creates a road map for the ideal parenting journey you both want to have by establishing clear parenting and relationship goals. Being on the same page is vital to successfully navigating this, many times, treacherous season of life. And when you feel like you're struggling, revisiting the parenting vision you created together can help you become the parent you want to be.

In this chapter, I'm going to walk you through the brainstorming and writing process so that in the end, you have a clear set of parenting and relationship goals, a family mission statement, and a group of parenting vows that will guide you through parenthood. And because writing it all out is a vital part of this process, I'll include several fill-in-the-blank statements and note-taking sections in the pages that follow.

Step One: How Do You Cope with Stress?

The first part of this process involves talking with one another and identifying strategies that help each of your de-stress. How do you like to de-stress? Do you need quiet time or do you like to do an activity? Do you like to be alone or with certain people? Does talking to someone help you downregulate your stress or do you just want to snuggle? Clearly, you probably have different coping strategies for different kinds of experiences. Listing them all out here and sharing them with your partner can really come in handy when the stress arrives.

To help you brainstorm ideas for your list, I asked my Instagram followers to submit their favorite ways to destress and here are some of their responses: go for a run, sleep, go out for drinks with someone, go golfing, get outside, sit in the sun, call my mom, get a pedicure/manicure, go shopping, drink coffee in peace, do a craft project, snuggle with my boyfriend, watch a movie at home with friends, share a bottle of wine with my bestie and talk about it, color, listen to my favorite music, take a shower, play racket ball, talk to my best friend about it, and go to the gym. Whatever your coping strategies are, it is important to keep them in mind and actually use them when baby-induced stress begins. The two of you should also know each other's favorite stress-reducing. When your partner is feeling stressed or overwhelmed with the transition to parenthood, encourage them to enact one of their own stress-reducing strategies.

Your Preferred Coping Strategies

_____

_____

_____

_____

_____

_____

_____

Your Partner's Preferred Coping Strategies

_____

_____

_____

_____

_____

_____

_____

Step Two: Parenting Goals

Think about the conversations you've had together up to this point. If you're getting ready to become a parent for the first time, this is an extremely exciting season in your life, filled with idealized perceptions and expectations. Think about all of those things. If you already have other children, think about what you think has been working and not working so far. And then contemplate the following questions. Ideally, what kind of parent do you want to be? What kind of parent do you know you do not want to be? Imagine that your child is 12; how would you like them to describe you?

Below is a list of a few dozen descriptors to get you brainstorming. Look these over with your partner. Circle the 5 that are most important to you and then in a different color pen, have your partner circle the 5 that are most important to them.

Strict	Judgmental	Reasonable	Compassionate
Authority	Strong	Proud	Understanding
Honest	Fun	Beautiful	Bossy
Critical	Brave	Hard-Working	Spontaneous
Affectionate	Organized	Arrogant	Emotional
Flexible	Caring	Inspiring	Vain
Selfish	Cool	Hilarious	Positive
Boring	Courageous	Disciplinarian	Faithful
Aggressive	Open	Angry	Determined
Adaptable	Trusting	Supportive	Adventurous
Inconsiderate	Sincere	Generous	Polite
Workaholic	Resourceful	Scary	Awesome
Frank	Inventive	Absent	Mean
Impatient	Loving	Exciting	Unpredictable
Easy	Lenient	Happy	Friendly

Now take those same color pens and cross off the 5 that you do not want to be part of who you are as a parent and have your partner cross off the 5 that they do not want to be part of who they are as a parent. And remember, agreeing on everything here is not always such a great idea. Children can definitely benefit from having two different parents who work together to guide them through life. It's not about you both being the same kind of parent as much as it is important for you to work together as a team. Complete the sentences below to include your 5 most desirable and 5 most undesirable descriptions.

FOR YOU: I want to be a parent who is:

I don't want to be a parent who is:

FOR YOUR PARTNER: I want to be a parent who is:

I don't want to be a parent who is:

What kinds of actions could you take to fulfill your desire to be the kind of parent you just described? Remember, these are actions you're going to strive for; not necessarily actions you will be capable of enacting every second of everyday. Be gentle with yourself. As Lelia Schott, parenting expert, has said, "No parent is always conscious, gentle, positive, peaceful, and authentic. We have to CHOOSE to be and practice moment by moment… day after day. The more we practice, the stronger we grow."

Maybe you think it's really important to listen, play, and snuggle to become the kind of parent you want to be. Or you think attending all of your children's plays, recitals, sport games, hobbies, and performances will help you develop into your version of the ideal parent. Think about all of the things your parent(s) did or didn't do that you enjoyed. Add these behaviors to your list. Look carefully at the descriptions you chose on the previous pages. What kinds of behaviors should you be doing to become that person? You're not to be able to write out every single behavior you ever hope to enact, but you can focus on a few that you think are vital to achieving your goals.

FOR YOU	FOR YOUR PARTNER
As a parent, I hope to…	As a parent, I hope to…

Use these personal choices to guide the way you create a clear set of parenting vows together. Speaking of guiding, before we get to writing your parenting vows, I want you to think about your shared (yes, you should work towards agreeing on this one) idea for the overall purpose of parenting. For instance, some believe that the purpose of parenting is to raise functional adults, while others believe the purpose of parenting is to shelter their children from experiencing hardship, and still others believe that parents should simply strive to keep their children alive. Your parenting purpose doesn't need to be complicated. It should serve as a handy reminder to yourself when you're in the heat of the moment that you're making the right decision. The simpler the purpose, the more effective it will be.

Think about what you both want YOUR parenting purpose to be and write it out together. In case this activity is proving to be a bit difficult for you, here are a few sample parenting purposes to help you brainstorm about your own.

To raise children into adults who
don't have to heal from their childhood.

To raise independent humans who are
ready to face the world on their own.

To create secure adults who feel safe and confident
because they view themselves positively, others as good-
intentioned, and the world as a great place to be.

To help our little people grow into big people
who are respectful, obedient, and polite.

Our parenting purpose is to:

Step Three: Relationship Goals

If you're married and took a pre-marital counseling course, you've probably already done a lot of the exercises I'm going to ask you to do in the following pages, but it never hurts to revisit of these ideas.

And if you've never done some of these activities, it doesn't matter how long you've been with your partner, it's always a great idea to write some of this stuff out and share it with your partner.

Start thinking about your relationship with this amazing person you're created this wonderful life with. Now start thinking about the answer to these questions:

- What have you enjoyed most up to this point? What has been the hardest part up to this point?
- What do you like most about your relationship? What could you do without?
- Ideally, what kind of romantic partner do you want to be? What kind of spouse do you know you do not want to be? Imagine that someone asked your partner to describe you; what do you hope they would include in their description?
- What kinds of actions would you love to typically enact with your partner? What kinds of behaviors would you hate to use with your partner?
- What aspects of your future do you think could become a problem in your relationship? How would you like to work through those issues?
- What's the BIG picture when it comes to the kind of partner you want to be for the person you love?

With these things in mind, complete the following sentences.

FOR YOU: I want to be a partner who

FOR YOUR PARTNER: I want to be a partner who

Now, I'm going to challenge you to look into the future. What do you ultimately hope for your relationship? Marriage, more children, living in another state together, starting a business together, owning a primary residence home or vacation home together, traveling the country/world, and/or enjoying your old age together?

FOR YOU	FOR YOUR PARTNER
Future relationship goals	Future relationship goals

Use the ideas you have developed for the kind of partner you want to be and keep the future goals you have for your relationship in mind when creating a shared relationship purpose. Just like your parenting purpose, your relationship purpose doesn't need to be complicated.

Think about what you both want YOUR relationship purpose to be and write it out together. Here are a few sample relationship purposes to help you brainstorm about your own.

> To always work towards connecting so that we can learn to truly empathize with each other's life experiences.

> To grow old and enjoy the family that we create together.

> To be adventurous and take risks to keep the excitement alive.

> To stay committed to always communicating with love and respect so that we can address conflict and grow closer.

Our relationship purpose is to:

Step Four: Your Vows

Reflecting on everything you've talked about and written down up to this point, I now want you to work on creating some vows; a set of promises you want to make to your partner as you start this new phase of life together (whether it's your first our fourth child). Just as couples who marry make public promises to love and cherish one another through thick and thin, I truly believe that parents should also create a set of their own vows related to maintaining their relationship through parenthood.

Think about the kind of romantic partner you want to be and the kind of parent you want to be. Think about the kind of family you want to have and about all of the bumps in the road you're destined to experience. And think about how you plan to deal with the stress of life. Write your own vows. Have your partner write their own vows.

They can be serious or silly; hopeful or realistic; meaningful or less significant. Write it all out.

For example, one of the vows that my husband and I have is that we promise to not take anything too personally that we say to each other in the middle of the night; especially if a child is crying. When our son, Gavin, was an infant, he had reflux and was very colicky. His incessant crying and need to be carried in a certain way, most of the day and night was terribly challenging. The amount of attention that he demanded was difficult for my husband and I to deal with because we didn't always agree about how to best handle the situation (and we also had a second crying baby to soothe). Coupled with the sleep deprivation that we were both experiencing, my husband and I would get into stupid tiffs about all kinds of insignificant things related to our cranky son.

"I've been carrying him around all day;
what the hell have you done?"
(i.e. The Chore War)

"You're not holding him right. If you would
hold him like *this* he would stop screaming!"
(i.e. The Gatekeeping War)

"Stop getting annoyed by him! He's just a
baby! And his stomach hurts! He can't help it!"
(i.e. The War about Nothing)

These phrases (and several dozen others) were said by my husband and I many times. And they didn't help our marriage. We were angry at one another about things we couldn't control. It was ridiculous. So, we vowed to not only work towards using kinder words with one another, but to also realize that the middle-of-the-night, sleep-deprived, stress-induced communication interactions we were having were not worth getting offended or infuriated by. The good news is that, as I've said, you eventually get out of this phase. The bad news is that some couples say or do things during this phase that negatively and sometimes permanently change their relationship. The best advice I have here is to try to not sweat the small stuff. Maybe that's a good vow—I promise to not sweat the small stuff.

After you've written your vows, you need to figure out what to do with them. This is where things can get creative—or not. Decide how you want to share your vows with one another. It doesn't have to be some big production. Over dinner, privately in your home, in front of loved ones, or in the delivery room—anything will be perfect. But please, share your vows. Out loud. To each other. And then keep your vows in a special place. Return to them when parenthood makes you weary or when you've slammed the door after an argument with the person you love or when you're sad about something your partner said. Remember the person you were when all you wanted in the whole wide world was the life that you have right now. The life that you dreamed of for years. And then get back to it. Don't give up.

I've heard many relationship researchers and experts (including myself) say over the years that relationships have rather consistent phases. To a certain extent, the first stage of relationships is filled with love, excitement, adventure, being mildly annoyed by your differences, and being relatively happy-go-lucky for a few to several years. The second stage is characterized by being mildly perturbed to seriously angry about each other's communication patterns and character flaws, potentially causing mild to severe conflict for a few years. Did I mention that most people have these adorable little stress-producers called children during the second phase? It's not always a fun-filled phase. The third phase is where both partners tend to be chill about it all because they've finally realized what's important in life and they've stopped caring about all of the bullshit that they fought about so intensely before. And sometimes, these phases repeat a few times over the course of a long-lasting relationship. Unfortunately, lots of couples never make it to that more peaceful third stage. They give up on their partner, themselves, or their life together. If you've both committed yourselves to this relationship, do it. Commit yourself to always work it out. Commit yourself to try everything. Commit yourself to love your partner through it all.

I know, you still have those pesky vows to write. Well, get to it.

Conclusion

Phew! That was a lot of work on your part! From learning about the five common arguments parents tend to have to gaining some serious perspective about how you and your partner's past impacts you now to developing a clear set of vows, I hope that this book has made you feel ready to tackle this whole parenting thing.

This next thing you're about to read is a bit controversial and I even considered not including it in this book. But I believe in it and it's been really helpful to lot of people, so fuck it. Here goes nothing.

Put your romantic relationship first. Before the kids, before your job, before your parents, before running your household, before it all. Why? Let me indulge you with my stove metaphor. The way I see it, most of us have several "pots" in our lives that we have to cook on a proverbial stove at the same time. You have a pot for your job, a pot for your house, one for your kids, one for your marriage, a pot for your volunteer work, one for your extended family, and one for any other significant roles you play in your life. Most of us also only have a four-burner stovetop with two burners in the front and two in the back. And, I personally believe that it is impossible for us to focus a significant amount of our time and energy on more than a couple of things at once. This means that some of our life's "pots" have to be put on the proverbial back burner; even if it is just for a short amount of time. And sometimes, we might even have to put a pot on the counter for a bit.

Something that I've learned over the years is that you have to work really hard at not putting your romantic partner on the back burner. You can put your children on the back burner (they're more resilient than you think; especially if you've helped them develop secure attachment foundations), you can put your job on the back burner (maybe learn to say "no" to a new project?), and you can put managing your household on the back burner (the dishes can wait). But your relationship with the person you are creating this wonderful life with has to stay on one of the front burners. So, what do you do with all of your other pots? The trick is to disperse the back burner and countertop suffering equally. Rotate those other pots while keeping your relationship on one of the front burners. Because if your romantic relationship fails, the rest will could easily follow suit. Eventually.

Resources

Thanks for reading my book! If you want even more information about healthy relationships, parenting, and constructive conflict, here's my approved-by-me book list! And below all of these excellent book choices, I've also included my favorite Instagram accounts that I think all parents should follow; both to help them be the best individuals, parents, and romantic partners they can be.

Books On Healthy Parenting...

The Attachment Connection: Parenting a Secure & Confident Child Using the Science of Attachment Theory by Ruth P. Newton, Ph.D.

Raising a Secure Child: How Circle of Security Parenting Can Help You Nurture Your Child's Attachment, Emotional Resilience, and Freedom to Explore by Kent Hoffman, Glen Cooper, and Bert Powell

Any book by Rebecca Eanes
- *The Gift of a Happy Mother: Letting Go of Perfection and Embracing Everyday Joy*
- *Positive Parenting: Ending the Power Struggles and Reconnecting from the Heat*
- *The Newbie's Guide to Positive Parenting*

The Happiest Baby on the Block: The New Way to Calm Crying and Help Your Newborn Baby Sleep Longer by Harvey Karp, M.D.

The 5 Love Languages of Children by Gary Chapman, Ph.D. & Ross Campbell, M.D.

Our Babies, Ourselves: How Biology and Culture Shape the Way We Parent by Meredith F. Small

The Whole-Brain Child: Revolutionary Strategies to Mature Your Child's Developing Mind by Daniel J. Siegel, M.D. & Tina Payne Bryson, Ph.D.

Raising an Emotionally Intelligent Child by John M. Gottman, Ph.D.

How to Talk So Kids Will Listen & Listen So Kids Will Talk by Adele Faber & Elaine Mazlish

Discipline Without Damage: How to Get Kids to Behave Without Messing Them Up by Vanessa LaPointe, R. Psych.

The Gentle Parent: Positive, Practical, Effective Discipline by L.R. Knost

Kids These Days: A Game Plan for (Re)Connecting with Those We Teach, Lead, & Love by Jody Carrington, Ph.D.

The Self-Driven Child: The Science and Sense of Giving Your Kids More Control Over Their Lives by William Stixrud, Ph.D., & Ned Johnson

Books On Healthy Romantic Relationships...

Attached: The New Science of Adult Attachment and How It Can Help You Find—And Keep—Love by Amir Levine, M.D. & Rachel Heller, M.A.

The 5 Love Languages by Gary Chapman, Ph.D.

Any John M. Gottman, Ph.D., book
- *What Makes Love Last? How to Build Trust and Avoid Betrayal*
- *The Seven Principles for Making Marriage Work: A Practical Guide from the Country's Foremost Relationship Expert*
- *Eight Dates: Conversations for a Lifetime of Love*
- *The Science of Trust: Emotional Attunement for Couples*
- *And Baby Makes Three: The Six-Step Plan for Preserving Marital Intimacy and Rekindling Romance After Baby Arrives*

Anxious in Love: How to Manage Your Anxiety, Reduce Conflict, & Reconnect with Your Partner by Carolyn Daitch, Ph.D. & Lissah Lorberbaum, M.A.

Avoidant: How to Love (Or Leave) a Dismissive Partner by Jeb Kinnison

Insecure in Love: How Anxious Attachment Can Make You Feel Jealous, Needy, and Worried and What You Can Do About It by Leslie Becker-Phelps, Ph.D.

Love That Works: A Guide to Enduring Intimacy by Wendy Strgar

Project Happily Ever After: Saving Your Marriage When the Fair Tale Falters by Alisa Bowman

Books On Constructive Conflict...

Fight Less, Love More: 5-Minute Conversations to Change Your Relationship without Blowing Up or Giving In by Laurie Puhn, J.D.

Wired for Love: How Understanding Your Partner's Brain and Attachment Style Can Help You Diffuse Conflict and Build a Secure Relationship by Stan Tatkin, PsyD, MFT

No More Fighting: The Relationship Book for Couples: 20 Minutes a Week to a Stronger Relationship by Alicia Muñoz

Last, but not least is my first book—***Make Love, Not Scrapbooks: And 9 Other Research-Based Love Tips to Intensify Your Relationship***

Instagram Accounts to Follow...

Before I get into my favorites, I clearly think you all should follow MY Instagram account: @RelationshipsLoveHappiness!

@RebeccaEanes

@TheDanishWay

@RaisedGood

@LRKnost

@Peaceful_Parenting

@TheShrinkWrap

@DuffThePsych

@SitWithSharon

@LoveProjectLove

@DrKaitlin

@IntentionalMarriages

@Dr.VanessaLaPointe

@GottmanInstitute

@EarlyOnMichigan

@Saia.org.uk

@TheApologyExpert

@HelloDrJoy

@HolisticallyGrace

@BreneBrown

@KidsAreTheWorst

@RaisingGoodHumans

@Hand_In_Hand_Parenting

@HolisticParentingMag

@Imago_Relationships

@DrJodyCarrington

@AustralianPsychologist

@Synergy.Gentle.Parenting

@LongestShortestTime

@TheGentleMama

@ProjectHappiness_org

@TinyHumansBigEmotions

@Beyond_Sleep_Training_Project

@Surviving_Toxic_Families

@ASafePlaceInsideYourHead

@5LoveLanguages

@Authentic.Parenting.Podcast

@PeacefulMindPeacefulLife

@LizListens

@AZPsychologist

@PowerofPositivity

References

[1] Cox, M. J., Paley, B., Burchinal, M., & Payne, C. C. (1999). Marital perceptions and interactions across the transition to parenthood. *Journal of Marriage and the Family, 61*(3), 611-625. Shapiro, A. F., Gottman, J. M., & Carrère, S. (2000). The baby and the marriage: Identifying factors that buffer against decline in marital satisfaction after the first baby arrives. *Journal of Family Psychology, 14*(1), 59-70. Lawrence, E., Nylen, K., & Cobb, R. J. (2007). Prenatal expectations and marital satisfaction over the transition to parenthood. *Journal of Family Psychology, 21*(2), 155-164. Schulz, M. S., Cowan, C. P., & Cowan, P. A. (2006). Promoting healthy beginnings: A randomized controlled trial of a preventative intervention to preserve marital quality during the transition to parenthood. *Journal of Counseling and Clinical Psychology, 74*(1), 20-31.

[2] Shapiro, A. F., Gottman, J. M., & Carrère, S. (2000). The baby and the marriage: Identifying factors that buffer against decline in marital satisfaction after the first baby arrives. *Journal of Family Psychology, 14*(1), 59-70.

[3] Cox, M. J., Paley, B., Burchinal, M., & Payne, C. C. (1999). Marital perceptions and interactions across the transition to parenthood. *Journal of Marriage and the Family, 61*(3), 611-625.

[4] Belsky, J. (1985). Exploring individual differences in marital change across the transition to parenthood: The role of violated expectations. *Journal of Marriage and Family, 47*(4), 1037-1044.

[5] Belsky, J., & Pensky, E. (1988). Marital change across the transition to parenthood. *Marriage & Family Review, 12*(3-4), 133–156.

[6] Shapiro, A. F., Gottman, J. M., & Carrère, S. (2000). The baby and the marriage: Identifying factors that buffer against decline in marital satisfaction after the first baby arrives. *Journal of Family Psychology, 14*(1), 59-70.

[7] Lawrence, E., Nylen, K., & Cobb, R. J. (2007). Prenatal expectations and marital satisfaction over the transition to parenthood. *Journal of Family Psychology, 21*(2), 155-164.

[8] Bowlby, J. (1969). *Attachment (Attachment and loss, Vol 1)*. New York: Basic Books. Bowlby, J. (1973). *Separation: Anxiety and anger*

(Attachment and loss, Vol. 2). New York: Basic Books. Bowlby, J. (1979). *The making and breaking of affectional bonds*. London, England: Tavistock.

[9] Bowlby, J. (1969). *Attachment (Attachment and loss, Vol 1)*. New York: Basic Books. Bowlby, J. (1973). *Separation: Anxiety and anger (Attachment and loss, Vol. 2)*. New York: Basic Books. Bowlby, J. (1979). *The making and breaking of affectional bonds*. London, England: Tavistock.

[10] Buckingham, D., & Bragg, S. (2003). Young people, media, and personal relationships. Chernin, A. R., & Fishbein, M. (2007, May). *The association between adolescents' exposure to romantic-themed media and the endorsement of unrealistic beliefs about romantic relationships*. Paper presented at the annual meeting of the International Communication Association. San Francisco, CA. Westman, A. S., Lynch, T. J., Lewandowski, L., & Hunt-Carter, E. (2003). Students' use of mass media for ideas about romantic relationships was influenced by perceived realism of presentations and parental happiness. *Psychological Reports, 92*(3), 1116-1118.

[11] Belsky, J., & Kelly, J. (1994). *The transition to parenthood: How a first child changes a marriage*. Vermillion. Cox, M. J., Paley, B., Burchinal, M., & Payne, C. C. (1999). Marital perceptions and interactions across the transition to parenthood. *Journal of Marriage and the Family, 61*(3), 611-625.

[12] Schultz, J. R., & Vaughn, L. M. (1999). Brief report: Learning to parent: A survey of parents in an urban pediatric primary care clinic. *Journal of Pediatric Psychology, 24*(5), 441-445. Young, K. T., Davis, K., Schoen, C., & Parker, S. (1998). Listening to parents: A national survey of parents with young children. *Archives of Pediatrics and Adolescent Medicine, 152*(3), 255-262.

[13] Plantin, L., & Daneback, K. (2009). Parenthood, information and support on the internet: A literature review of research on parents and professionals online. *BMC Family Practice, 10*(34), 10-34.

[14] Crawford, M. (2007). *When two become three: Nuturing your marriage after baby arrives*. Ada, MI: Revell.

[15] Blair, S. L., & Johnson, M. P. (1992). Wives' perceptions of the fairness of the division of household labor: The intersection of housework and ideology. *Journal of Marriage and the Family, 54*, 570-581. Demo, D. H., & Acock, A. C. (1993). Family diversity and the division of domestic labor: How much have things really

changed? *Family Relations, 42,* 323-331. Hawkins, A. J., Marshall, C. M. and Allen, S. M. (1998). The orientation toward domestic labor questionnaire: Exploring dual-earner wives' sense of fairness about family work. *Journal of Family Psychology, 12*(2), 244-258.

[16] Sokol, R. I., Webster, K. L., Thompson, N. S., & Stevens, D. A. (2005). Whining as mother-directed speech. *Infant and Child Development, 14,* 478-490.

[17] Chang, R. S. & Thompson, N. S. (2011). Whines, cries, and motherese: Their relative power to distract. *Journal of Social, Evolutionary, and Cultural Psychology, 5*(2), 131-141.

[18] Deutsch, F. (1999). *Having it all: How equally shared parenting works.* Cambridge, MA: Harvard University Press.

[19] Rupp, H. A., James, T. W., Ketterson, E. D., Senegelaub, D. R., Ditzen, B., & Heiman, J. R. (2013). Lower sexual interest in postpartum women: Relationship to amygdala activation and intranasal oxytytocin. *Hormones and Behavior, 63*(1), 114-121.

[20] Rupp, H. A., James, T. W., Ketterson, E. D., Senegelaub, D. R., Ditzen, B., & Heiman, J. R. (2013). Lower sexual interest in postpartum women: Relationship to amygdala activation and intranasal oxytytocin. *Hormones and Behavior, 63*(1), 114-121.

[21] Barrett, G., Pendry, E., Peacock, J., Victor, C., Thakar, R., & Manyonda, I. (2000). Women's sexual health after childbirth. *BJOG International Journal of Obstetrics and Gynaecology, 107*(2), 186–195. Leeman, L.M. & Rogers, R.G. (2012). Sex after childbirth: Postpartum sexual function. *Obstetrics Gynecology, 119*(3), 647–655. Glazener, C.M.A. (1997). Sexual function after childbirth: Women's experiences, persistent morbidity and lack of professional recognition. *Obstetrical Gynecological Survey, 52*(9), 529–530. Hicks, T.L., Goodall, S.F., Quattrone, E.M., & Lydon-Rochelle, M.T. (2004). Postpartum sexual functioning and method of delivery: Summary of the evidence. *Journal of Midwifery Women's Health, 49*(5), 430–436. Signorello, L.B., Harlow, B.L., Chekos, A.K., Repke, J.T. (2001). Postpartum sexual functioning and its relationship to perineal trauma: A retrospective cohort study of primiparous women. *American Journal of Obstetrics Gynecology, 184*(5), 881–890.

[22] O'Malley, D., Higgins, A., & Smith, V. (2000). Postpartum sexual health: A principle-based concept analysis. Journal of Advanced Nursing, 71(10), 2247–2257. Barrett, G., Pendry, E.,

Peacock, J., Victor, C., Thakar, R., & Manyonda, I. (2000). Women's sexual health after childbirth. *BJOG International Journal of Obstetrics and Gynaecology, 107*(2), 186–195.

[23] Barrett, G., Pendry, E., Peacock, J., Victor, C., Thakar, R., & Manyonda, I. (2000). Women's sexual health after childbirth. *BJOG International Journal of Obstetrics and Gynaecology, 107*(2), 186–195.

[24] Johnson, C. E. (2011). Sexual health during pregnancy and the postpartum. *Journal of Sex Medicine, 8*(5), 1267–1284.

[25] Rupp, H. A., James, T. W., Ketterson, E. D., Senegelaub, D. R., Ditzen, B., & Heiman, J. R. (2013). Lower sexual interest in postpartum women: Relationship to amygdala activation and intranasal oxytocin. *Hormones and Behavior, 63*(1), 114-121.

[26] McDonald, E., Woolhouse, H., Brown, S.J. (2015). Consultation about sexual health issues in the year after childbirth: A cohort study. *Birth, 42*(4), 354–361.

[27] Barrett, G., Pendry, E., Peacock, J., Victor, C., Thakar, R., & Manyonda, I. (2000). Women's sexual health after childbirth. *BJOG International Journal of Obstetrics and Gynaecology, 107*(2), 186–195.

[28] LaMarre, A., Paterson, L., & Gorzalka, B. (2003). Breastfeeding and postpartum sexual functioning: A review. *Canadian Journal of Human Sexuality, 12*(3–4), 151–168. Barrett, G., Pendry, E., Peacock, J., Victor, C., Thakar, R., & Manyonda, I. (2000). Women's sexual health after childbirth. *BJOG International Journal of Obstetrics and Gynaecology, 107*(2), 186–195. Johnson, C. E. (2011). Sexual health during pregnancy and the postpartum. *Journal of Sex Medicine, 8*(5), 1267–1284.

[29] Rowland, M., Foxcroft, L., Hopman, W. M., & Patel, R. (2005). Breastfeeding and sexuality immediately post partum. *Canadian Family Physician, 51*(10), 1367-1372.

[30] LaMarre, A., Paterson, L., & Gorzalka, B. (2003). Breastfeeding and postpartum sexual functioning: A review. *Canadian Journal of Human Sexuality, 12*(3–4), 151–168.

[31] McBride, H. & Kwee, J. (2016). Focusing on the mother in maternal health care: A review of perinatal mental health needs and promising interventions. *The Journal of Psychological Therapies in Primary Care, 5*, 1–25.

[32] McBride, H. & Kwee, J. (2016). Focusing on the mother in maternal health care: A review of perinatal mental health needs

and promising interventions. *The Journal of Psychological Therapies in Primary Care, 5*, 1–25. Gawley, L., Einarson, A., & Bowen, A. (2011). Stigma and attitudes towards antenatal depression and antidepressant use during pregnancy in healthcare students. *Advanced Health Science Education, 16*(5), 669–679. Goodman, J.H. & Santangelo, G. (2011). Group treatment for postpartum depression: A systematic review. *Archives of Women's Mental Health, 14*(4), 277–293. Zaers, S., Waschke, M., & Ehlert, U. (2008). Depressive symptoms and symptoms of post-traumatic stress disorder in women after childbirth. *Journal of Psychosomatic Obstetric Gynecology, 29*(1), 61–71.

[33] Pastore, L., Owens, A., & Raymond, C. (2006). Postpartum sexuality concerns among first-time parents from one U.S. academic hospital. *The Journal of Sexual Medicine, 4*(1), 115-123.

[34] Condon, J., Boyce, P., & Corkindale, C. (2004). The first-time fathers study: A prospective study of the mental health and wellbeing of men during the transition to parenthood. *Australian New Zealand Journal of Psychiatry, 38*(1–2), 56–64.

[35] Olsson, A., Robertson, E., Björklund, A., & Nissen, E. (2010). Fatherhood in focus, sexual activity can wait: new fathers' experience about sexual life after childbirth. *Scandinavian Journal of Caring Sciences, 24*(4), 716–725.

[36] Whipple, B., Knowles, J., & Davis, J. (2007). *The health benefits of sexual expression.* White Paper published by the Katharine Dexter McCormick Library Planned Parenthood Federation of America.

[37] Palmore, E. (1982). Predictors of the longevity difference: A twenty-five year follow-up. *The Gerontologist, 22*, 513- 518. Smith, D. S., Frankel, S., & Yarnell, J. (1997). Sex and death: Are they related? *British Medical Journal, 314*, 1641-1645.

[38] Gallup, G., Burch, R. L., & Platek, S. M. (2002). Does semen have antidepressant properties? *Archives of Sexual Behavior, 31*, 289-293.

[39] Hurlbert, D. F., & Whittaker, K. E. (1991). The role of masturbation in marital and sexual satisfaction: A comparative study of female masturbators and nonmasturbators. *Journal of Sex Education & Therapy, 17*, 272- 282.

[40] Odent, M. (1999). *The scientification of love.* London, UK: Free Association Books Limited. Weeks, D. J. (2002). Sex for the amateur adult: Health, self-esteem and countering ageist stereotypes. *Sexual and Relationship Therapy, 17*, 231- 240.

[41] Fitness, J. (2001). Betrayal, rejection, revenge, and forgiveness: An interpersonal script approach. In M.R. Leary (Ed.). *Interpersonal rejection*, (pp. 73-103). New York: Oxford University Press.

[42] Cutrona, C. E. (1996). Social support as a determinant of marital quality: The interplay of negative and supportive behaviors. In G. R. Pierce, B. R. Sarason, & I. G. Sarason (Eds.). *Handbook of social support and the family*. New York: Plenam Press.

[43] Birchler, G. R., Weiss, R. L., & Vincent, J. P. (1975). Multimethod analysis of social reinforcement exchange between maritally distressed and nondistressed spouse and stranger dyads. *Journal of Personality and Social Psychology, 31*, 349-360. Gottman, J. M. (1979). *Marital interaction: Experimental investigations*. New York: Academic Press. Margolin, G., & Wompold, B. E. (1981). A sequential analysis of conflict and accord in distressed and nondistressed marital partners. *Journal of Consulting and Clinical Psychology, 49*, 554- 557.

[44] Gottman, J. M. (1979). *Marital interaction: Experimental investigations*. New York: Academic Press.

[45] Prager, J. K. (1995). *The psychology of intimacy*. New York: Guilford Press.

[46] Doohan, E.-A., M., & Manusov, V. (2004). The communication of compliments in romantic relationships: An investigation of relational satisfaction and sex differences and similarities in compliment behavior. *Western Journal of Communication, 68*, 170-194. Prager, J. K. (1995). *The psychology of intimacy*. New York: Guilford Press.

[47] Doohan, E.-A., M., & Manusov, V. (2004). The communication of compliments in romantic relationships: An investigation of relational satisfaction and sex differences and similarities in compliment behavior. *Western Journal of Communication, 68*, 170-194.

[48] Wolfson, N., & Manes, J. (1980). The compliment as a social strategy. *Papers in Linguistics: International Journal of Human Communication, 13*, 391-410.

[49] Gaunt, R. & Pinho, M. (2018). Do sexist mothers change more diapers? Ambivalent sexism, maternal gatekeeping, and the division of childcare. *Sex Roles, 79*, 176-189.

[50] Claxton, A. & Perry-Jenkins, M. (2008). No fun anymore: Leisure and marital quality across the transition to parenthood. *Journal of Marriage and Family, 70*(1), 28-43.

[51] Aron, A., Norman, C., Aron, E., McKenna, C., & Heyman, R. (2000). Couples' shared participation in novel and arousing activities and experienced relationship quality. *Journal of Personality and Social Psychology, 78*, 273-284.

[52] Cummings, E. M., & Davies, P. T. (2010). *Marital conflict and children: An emotional security perspective.* New York: Guilford Press.

[53] Schofield, T. J., Conger, R. D., Gonzales, J. E., & Merrick, M. T. (2016). Harsh parenting, physical health, and the protective role of positive parent-adolescent relationships. *Social Science & Medicine, 157*, 18-26.

[54] Corry, B. (1992). *Understanding domestic violence: A recovery resource for battered women and those who work with them.* Care Program.

[55] Cynthia Henrie, MFT

[56] See Steele & Shepard (2003) and Facts for Families (1999)

[57] Harvard Center for the Developing Child (2014). Retrieved from https://developingchild.harvard.edu/resources/wp3/

[58] Harvard Center for the Developing Child, 2014, p. 2

[59] (Bowlby, J. (1969). *Attachment (Attachment and loss, Vol 1).* New York: Basic Books. Bowlby, J. (1973). *Separation: Anxiety and anger (Attachment and loss, Vol. 2).* New York: Basic Books. Bowlby, J. (1979). *The making and breaking of affectional bonds.* London, England: Tavistock.

[60] Burleson, B. R. (2003). Emotional support skills. In J. O. Greene & B. R. Burleson (Eds.), *Handbook of communication and social interaction skills* (p. 551–594). Lawrence Erlbaum Associates Publishers.

[61] Rothwell, J. (2010). *In the company of others: An introduction to communication.* New York: Oxford University Press.

[62] Wilmot, W. W., & Hocker, J. L. (2007). *Interpersonal conflict.* New York: McGraw Hill. Lulofs, R. (1994). *Conflict: From theory to action.* Scottsdale, AZ: Gorsuch Scarisbrick.

[63] Fitness, J. (2001). Betrayal, rejection, revenge, and forgiveness: An interpersonal script approach. In M.R. Leary (Ed.). *Interpersonal rejection,* (pp. 73-103). New York: Oxford University Press.

[64] Cutrona, C. E. (1996). Social support as a determinant of marital quality: The interplay of negative and supportive behaviors. In G. R. Pierce, B. R. Sarason, & I. G. Sarason (Eds.). *Handbook of social support and the family.* New York: Plenam Press.

[65] Birchler, G. R., Weiss, R. L., & Vincent, J. P. (1975). Multimethod analysis of social reinforcement exchange between maritally distressed and nondistressed spouse and stranger dyads.

Journal of Personality and Social Psychology, 31, 349-360. Gottman, J. M. (1979). *Marital interaction: Experimental investigations.* New York: Academic Press. Margolin, G., & Wompold, B. E. (1981). A sequential analysis of conflict and accord in distressed and nondistressed marital partners. *Journal of Consulting and Clinical Psychology, 49*, 554- 557.

[66] Gottman, J. M. (1979). *Marital interaction: Experimental investigations.* New York: Academic Press.

[67] Gottman, J., & Silver, N. (1994). Why marriages succeed of fail: How you can make your last. New York: Simon & Schuster.

[68] Gottman & Silver, 1994, p. 80.

Made in the USA
Middletown, DE
11 October 2020